THE PRINCIPLES AND PRACTICE
OF RETREAT

THE PRINCIPLES AND PRACTICE OF RETREAT

BY THE

REV. ALAN H. SIMPSON, M.A.

*Canon Missioner, Diocese of Coventry ; Warden of the
Retreat House, Rugby ; General Secretary to the
Association for Promoting Retreats*

A. R. MOWBRAY & CO. Ltd.
London : 28 Margaret Street, Oxford Circus, W. 1
Oxford : 9 High Street
Milwaukee, U.S.A.: The Morehouse Publishing Co.
Printed in England

First impression, 1927

PREFACE

IT is hoped that this small book may go a little way towards meeting two needs that, at the moment, are of special importance.

In the first place the cause of Retreat is suffering from a certain vagueness and confusion of ideas. Many people are indeed awakening to the need of times of stillness. But all of them have not been put in the way of understanding the principles upon which a true Retreat depends, with the result that some find it difficult to reap the full benefits of the practice. The same cause, too, prevents many from realizing how great are the opportunities that the extension of Retreats is offering to the Church in our generation.

Secondly, an increasing number of the clergy are being asked to act as Conductors. Many of them are reluctant to accept the invitation because, even though they may have been into Retreat themselves, they are aware that there are important questions of method which they have had little opportunity of studying.

Both these classes of inquirers have been kept in mind throughout the following pages, and it may be that both will find therein some small measure of assistance.

ALAN H. SIMPSON

THE RETREAT HOUSE,
    RUGBY.
Michaelmas, 1927.

CONTENTS

PART ONE

THE PRINCIPLES OF RETREAT

PART TWO

THE CONDUCTING OF RETREATS

Contents

APPENDICES

PART ONE

THE PRINCIPLES OF RETREAT

CHAPTER I

RETREAT AND THE RELIGION OF THE BIBLE

IT is an easy line of appeal to urge people to go into Retreat on the grounds that in the rush of the world to-day they have so little leisure to consider the deeper things of life. Apostleship of the obvious, however, is seldom helpful to any movement ; and in this case, especially, it confuses principles and therefore tends to weaken the cause it is intended to support. For there is surely nothing we ought to be more anxious to dispel than the notion, already too common, that the Retreat is a modern device, to be commended chiefly as a means of counteracting the special difficulties of our age.

The real truth is so much more impressive and convincing. It is that the Retreat, new only in external form, is the embodiment of certain elements of spiritual experience that always have been, and always will be, necessary for the due realization of God by the human soul, and for the proper development of man's spiritual nature. Present conditions may indeed make the necessity of Retreat more urgent for most people than it has ever been before. But, since many minds are rightly enough suspicious of recently invented remedies for our present ills, nothing needs plainer statement than the main principle upon which the practice of Retreat really depends, namely, that the religion of the Bible is essentially a religion of knowledge of God ; and that a vital element in the acquiring of that knowledge is the experience of being alone, stripped from all concealments and freed from all distractions, in the realized presence of God. It could easily be shown, if space permitted, that many of our weaknesses and difficulties have come about through the habitual neglect of this principle.

There can be no doubt as to the witness of Holy Scripture. Retreat appears nowhere in its pages as a sort of spiritual luxury which specially busy people, or for that matter specially devout people, may seek if they feel so inclined. It is shown, rather, as the necessary opening of the

way for every life of service, and no less
as the refreshment of that life.   Here lies
the true association of the matter that
ought to be vividly in the mind of the
Church of our day, but which is apt to be
obscured by the shallower appeal.   The
recent growth of the practice of Retreat has
not come about simply because busy people
have been forced to seek times of quiet.
The truly important cause is that Christian
life is being more insistently taught as
essentially a life of service, and therefore
the real need of Retreat is being more
widely felt.

In the past there has been something
strangely inconsistent between our appeal
to Holy Scripture on the one hand, and,
on the other, our indifference to the importance of Retreat.   All through the Bible
there runs, as constantly as its witness to
the need of prayer, the setting forth of an
order of spiritual processes, declared to be
necessary for finding and sustaining the
power without which human life cannot
be devoted to the work of the kingdom of
God.   This order is not, as might be
supposed from much that we see in our
modern Church-life, discussion, organization, efficiency.   It is, rather, stillness,

vision, service. The soul called to serve is first led apart from the disquietudes of the world. In that stillness comes a vision of God's purpose ; of that vision is born the spirit of consecration.

This can be illustrated very easily from many parts of the Bible, and the reader is recommended to study carefully the passages suggested at the end of this chapter. It will be sufficient for the moment to dwell upon one instance taken from the Old Testament, and then to indicate the working of the truth in the earthly life of our Blessed Lord Himself.

Moses was called to the great venture, humanly speaking impossible, of delivering the people of God from the bondage of Egypt. But he was not required as a first step to cause a representative Exodus committee to be elected, with an influential chairman (one, if possible, who might carry weight even in court circles), and a capable and businesslike secretary to keep minutes and send resolutions about freedom to Pharaoh. Is it stretching a parable too violently to suggest that there are parishes where the people of God at the present day remain in something not unlike the bondage of Egypt, because such

ourse is the only one that occurs to
minds of their leaders ? Moses was
eed a great organizer ; but that was
:ause he had learned that organization
only the direction and never the source
power. First, before he took any
easures that would nowadays be called
actical, he was led to the step that, in
.ct, not only changed his whole life, but
ightily affected the history of the whole
orld. He was sent to the back side of
he desert, to Horeb the Mount of God.
n that stillness there came to him a revela-
:ion of God's purpose in the vision of the
Burning Bush ; and of that vision the
motive power was born that, we may almost
say, drove him out to the work he would
otherwise have shrunk from undertaking
at all.

In the New Testament the same truth
is witnessed nowhere more plainly than in
the record of the earthly life and ministry
of our Lord and Saviour Jesus Christ.
One of our difficulties at the present day
comes from an unconscious, but all too real,
mistrust in people's minds of the immediate effect of spiritual means on outward
conduct. Thus we are often told that we
must have a practical religion ; yet that

what the world needs is not an increase within the Church of ' hot-house ' devotion, but simply the witness of Christian men and women who follow the example of their Master in the ordinary ways of daily life.

One dare not say that the Church has given no occasion for this mistrust of its ways of devotion. Yet, when people speak like that, have they considered what in truth our Lord's example is like ? The Gospels do not declare to us only the outward life of going about doing good. They show us, at least in glimpses, the inner life which lay behind all that in Jesus Christ has commanded the admiration of men. We see as part of this background forty days of Retreat before the ministry begins. When it has begun, at the very times when the opportunities of the kingdom were most abundant, when crowds were coming from the towns and villages demanding His teaching, and bringing their sick to be healed, we see Him deeming it neither a waste of time, nor a turning aside from duty, to go into the wilderness, or up into the mountain, simply to be alone with God the Father.

The choosing of the Twelve was a critical occasion of the ministry. We read of our Lord preparing for that choice in a night of lonely vigil. Nor is it any less plain that He impressed upon the disciples this need of Retreat for their own lives of service. He led the three principal members of their body into the Retreat of the Transfiguration, where in stillness vision was granted that the spirit of service might be renewed. Again, He said to them all, 'Come ye apart into a desert place and rest a while.' But, what is most significant and yet seems to have been strangely missed in much that has been written about Retreat, it was by our Lord's own appointment that the Upper Room was placed at the disposal of the disciples. There in seclusion they heard the Last Discourses, and witnessed the Institution of the Eucharist. There, after the Resurrection and Ascension, they waited in prayer and supplication for the Day of Pentecost.

Surely we may rightly point to that as almost the most impressive scene in all human history ! Here were those few people, of no special powers or influence, charged with a work that on the face of it was hopeless. Yet they neither went back in despair to their fisher-homes in Galilee; nor did they rush out, in a sheer enthusiasm of loyalty to their Master, to do or die. They waited in Retreat, till the promise of their Lord's own gift had been fulfilled; and then, without hesitation or fear, they went out to fulfil His command.

Such is the record of the New Testament, or rather a very small part of it. When we consider it, do we not ask in amazement where did people ever get the notion that Retreat is a new invention, or that there is a practical form of Christianity that need take no account of it? Surely, if the Bible is to weigh with us at all, we can come only to one conclusion. If a man sincerely desires to follow the example of Jesus Christ, one of the first things required of him is to secure regular and frequent occasions when he can go apart, not for a few short minutes, but for hours and days, to be alone with God.

It is because this truth has been insufficiently realized that we have incurred much of the restlessness, shallowness, and want of confidence to be found in modern religion; it is to restore an indispensable element of the spiritual life that many are

now spending and being spent in further-
ing the cause of Retreat.

NOTE : The following passages should
be carefully studied by the reader, who
should note the different types and objects
of Retreat that are there recorded.

Genesis xxxii. 24; Exodus iii. 1 to iv. 17;
1 Kings xix. 1–18; Isaiah vi. 1–8; Ezekiel
i ; Daniel x ; Amos ; Jonah iv. 5–11 ;
Zechariah. S. Matthew iv ; S. Luke iv.
40–42, v. 15–16, vi. 12–13, ix. 28–36,
xxii. 11–13 ; S. Mark ; S. John ; Acts
i. 12–14 ; Galatians i. 17–18 ; Revelation i. 9–10, viii. 1–4.

CHAPTER II

THE PURPOSE OF RETREAT

RETREATS are of many kinds. There is the corporate Retreat, and the solitary Retreat. There is the critical Retreat, when some great issue of life is to be faced, or some momentous choice is to be made. There is the Retreat that is undertaken as a special preparation for some act, or way, of service. There is the periodic Retreat, that is intended for the reordering of life and the renewal of spiritual power.

All these types of Retreat have their place in Holy Scripture, and, at least to some extent, they are represented in the life of the Church to-day. Thus it might be said, and in a sense it would be true, that there are many and various purposes of Retreat.

Yet the truth that matters most is a far deeper one. It is that, underlying this diversity of objects, there is one main purpose, that must be express and direct, in all Retreats that are really worthy to be called by that name. It is that the Retreatants should be brought into a closer union with God, and a clearer understanding of His will for their own lives.

This may appear at first sight a statement too obvious to stand in need of emphasis. Yet, in fact, there is nothing in the whole question that requires to be insisted on more constantly. It is indeed the very point round which centres a confusion of ideas that is even now a great hindrance to the extension of Retreats. A large feature in the work of our Retreat Houses at the present day consists of gatherings to which people are invited, not so much in virtue of their personal relation to God, as because of their membership of some guild or association. These gatherings are quite commonly called Retreats, and no doubt sometimes with strict justice. But frequently they are really of the nature of conferences, or schools of instruction. For, even in cases where silence is observed, the subjects put forward for consideration do not relate directly to the personal life, but rather to the objects, or even the methods, of the organization to which the Retreatants belong.

No one, let it be said at once, wishes to urge that such a procedure in itself is wrong. It may very truly be claimed that an association is likely to derive great benefit from such a gathering; and, if it happens to resemble a Retreat in the observance of silence, that is probably all to the good. But it does need to be plainly stated that the object in such a case is by no means identical with that of Retreat. For the Retreat is not a conference or ' school,' and cannot be made to do duty as such without violence to its nature. The Retreat is a method of its own kind, and has a purpose which is distinct. It is essentially a mission to the soul, and it is concerned, directly, only with the interior ways of spiritual life. Until this is grasped more plainly and widely than it appears to be at present, especially by those who are in positions of leadership, there is a danger that the Retreat will continue to be regarded (as in the main it is at present) as merely a desirable side-issue in the Church's ministry. But when this one confusion is cleared up, then the Retreat will begin to be generally perceived in its true nature, namely, as a method which, in itself and for its own direct effects, is worth a concentration of effort (and if necessary the sacrifice of many less useful activities) in order to secure its rightful place in the very forefront of the Church's spiritual ministrations.

This claim for the importance of the Retreat can be quite simply justified. The Retreat is, of all spiritual methods, the one that goes most surely to the root of the soul's needs because its object is so fundamental. It deals with simplified causes of spiritual failure, and not, as do so many of our methods, with complicated symptoms. It is the cure of apathy and unreality, because it is the condition under which strong motive and sincerity most surely revive. It has, indeed, been well said that 'formal Churchmanship can hardly survive a well-kept Retreat.'

Here is a statement that is well worth a close examination because it takes us to the root of the whole matter. Few, probably, would care to deny that this 'formal Churchmanship,' or 'conventional religion,' is the most generally serious of all spiritual maladies. It is widespread, past calculation, insidious and subtle beyond description ; and, notoriously, it is the chief reason why the witness and message of the Church are apt to be discredited in the judgement of the world. When we ask what this most disastrous blight upon the religious life consists of, and how it comes to be so prevalent, a little care is needed in framing the answer.

Like every other spiritual weakness, it can be traced, of course, in the last resort to an interior loss of the soul's love for God. But when we examine into the course of its operation we find that it is something much more subtle than mere hypocrisy. It is but a hasty confusion of thought to identify conventionalism in the religious life with what is usually known as ' Pharisaism,' for it by no means necessarily proceeds from a desire to ' seem to be religious ' beyond what facts justify. The number of people, indeed, who go to church because they wish to appear better than others, or even think themselves to be so, is probably much smaller than the world is apt to suppose. It may even be alleged, judging from much of our popular literature, that there is more Pharisaism outside the Church at the present day than there is within it. But this 'conventional religion' of which the Church is indeed all too full comes, rather, from a disposition, into which even humble souls can fall, to turn aside from the high quest of the spiritual life and seek an easier line.

Contentment with forms arises from forgetfulness of the purpose for which those forms exist. There is a losing of the end in the means. People of almost any type can only too easily come to trust to the habits of religion, while all the time they are forgetting the one object which alone can make those habits worth pursuing. Thus they continue to make their communions, say their prayers, and join in worship, while they are losing that end for the sole attainment of which all means of grace have been provided, namely, the growing union of the soul with God in the Lord Jesus Christ. They forget that life eternal is knowledge of Him ; that all externals of religion whatsoever are senseless and useless but as the way of realizing the one thing which matters in all life, namely, the Divine Friendship. Thus the very system that should make for spiritual growth becomes, by perversion of use, the

c

aimless turnings of a soul-destroying machine.

Now it is true of any friendship, human or divine, that it tends to grow weak unless now and then times are *wholly* devoted to its interests. We may meet a person, with whom we have just begun a friendship, every day of our life. But if those meetings are always short, still more if they be always hurried, the friendship does not deepen. It may not even endure. Who does not know that frequent short conversations with the same person—in a tramcar, on the railway platform—may easily become embarrassing rather than fruitful ? They tend more and more to be restricted to the surface things of life— the headlines of the newspapers ; current politics ; a football match ; a joke. The friendship degenerates into mere formal acquaintance. We talk because we feel we ought to, rather than because we wish to reveal or to learn. The only safeguard is found in visits paid solely for the sake of closer knowledge of one's friend. If we are careful to secure times when we can really be with him, telling him about ourselves, attending as he discloses his mind to us, the reality of friendship is secure. Meaning is brought back into all other occasions of intercourse. A few words from a close friend, even in the street, a few short lines from him in a letter, mean infinitely more to us than the same things from a chance acquaintance could ever mean. The visits we have spent with him have revived that mutual self-revelation which is of the essence of friendship.

The analogy holds good in the spiritual life, and brings us to the truth which lies in the very heart of the purpose of Retreat. Conventional religion may be described quite justly as nothing else than ' formal acquaintance ' with God supplanting the Divine Friendship. The affairs of the world are pressing and insistent. Many people, long, perhaps, established in the ways of Church-life, are only too easily tempted to suppose that all is well, if in face of this pressure they maintain their habits of devotion and do not positively forsake the ways of grace. Thus they lose the end while pursuing only the means. They are far gone, often enough, from the reality of the Divine Friendship before they have been awakened to the fact that anything is amiss. No less often there are young people, at the beginning of spiritual experience, who have seen a glimpse of the possibility of the closer walk with God, and have vaguely, or even earnestly, desired it, but who have hardly found it yet as an actual and realized state. The ordinary practices of Christian life have perhaps been carefully explained to them, and insistently pressed upon them as a duty. Thus they find themselves committed to a scheme in which the means loom so large that the end may all too easily become obscured. They have just lacked the opportunity of a deeper way of first-hand knowledge that would secure reality and satisfaction.

Thus in the past, through the silence in our teaching concerning Retreat, we have withheld from both these sorts of people the way of attaining an essential element of the spiritual life. We have in consequence shut out the jaded from the surest way of recovery, and the beginners from the most hopeful way of growing realization. We have made more imminent for both the risk of formal religion—or even the final disaster of drift.

The Retreat, then, expressed in its simplest terms is a special visit that we pay to God, in order to know Him better. Its purpose is to revive within ourselves a sense of real union with God. But it must ever be remembered that, normally, souls are called apart into Retreat, not that they may remain apart, marked off from other Christians in a special way of devotion (Guilds of Retreatants, for instance, may become a real danger if they are made to suggest a sort of spiritual aristocracy), but that they may go back and find revived reality in the ordinary ways of grace and worship, witness and service.

It is because this renewing of the sense of God's real concern with the soul is the key to all that is vital in religion that the Retreat stands out now among all our methods as that which touches most closely the root of all our problems. For the Retreat brings to souls that re-conviction from within, apart from which insistent appeals from without are powerless to break down the barriers of apathy. If we could face the opportunity now, as our forefathers faced the call of education; if we could provide Retreat Houses, as they more than provided schools, at least on the scale of one for each of our great towns in England, in two generations we should see a Church renewed in vision and power—and that would be a long way towards seeing a nation with a changing conception of the need and the meaning of the Christian religion.

CHAPTER III

THE SECLUSION OF RETREAT

THE Retreat House, because of the rigour of our northern climate, takes with us the place that the Desert and the Mount are seen to occupy in Holy Scripture. A question therefore often presents itself to the minds of parish priests who are anxious to increase for their people opportunities of devotion, and yet hesitate to advise them to face the difficulty and cost of a visit to the nearest Retreat House. Could not the same purpose, they ask, be fulfilled by means which lie readier to hand ? Cannot people be gathered together for the space of two or three days in the church, or some other parish building, and be allowed to return to their homes just for the times that are necessary for meals and sleep ? This, too, clearly opens up a further question of great practical importance to the extension of the work, namely, is there really need for so large a number of Retreat Houses as advocates of the method appear to demand ?

In answering these questions we should be careful to avoid two opposite errors. We need not make the good appear as the enemy of the best ; but we must not encourage hopes, that are ill founded, of finding an easy and comparatively costless way of grasping the opportunity which is being offered by the growing desire for Retreats.

First, therefore, let it be readily admitted that good results of a kind may certainly be achieved by what is known as the ' open ' Retreat, provided very careful arrangements are made to secure as far as possible an atmosphere of stillness. Yet even here a warning is necessary against the confusion that is sometimes introduced into the question by the proposal of a ' Quiet Day.' The Quiet Day is not simply a short Retreat. It is something of a different nature, and the attempt to conduct it in the manner of a Retreat is to lose sight of its proper object. A rough illustration will serve best to show the distinction. It is one thing to anchor a ship in some quiet creek for a short respite from the wind and waves. It is quite

another matter to ' careen ' a vessel for
the purpose of cleaning the hull, repairing
the rigging, and stopping the leaks. No
amount of repetition of the former operation can dispense with the need of the
latter.

Thus a Quiet Day is not a Retreat
because, being too short for an examination and reordering of life, its use should
be simply for refreshment. It is dangerous, too, to assume that the experience of
a Quiet Day necessarily leads people to a
desire for Retreat. In the case of young
folk, at least, it often has exactly the opposite effect, since many of them find a few
hours of silence long enough to be tedious,
but too short to carry them on to a realization of the joy and benefits of stillness.
Experienced Retreatants, on the other
hand, will commonly be found appreciative
of occasional Quiet Days.

But the danger of making the good the
enemy of the best is, after all, neither so
grave or so widespread as that of attempt-
ing to substitute easier plans for difficult
ventures, and deluding ourselves that
nothing is lost in the result. Hence it
needs to be stated quite plainly that the
' open ' Retreat, even at its best, cannot be

expected to produce the effects, often so astonishing, of even a short Retreat in the full sense of the term. The reason is simple ; it is that the ' open ' Retreat is bound to be seriously deficient in the necessary element of complete and unbroken seclusion from the ordinary surroundings of life.

To argue thus that certain conditions must be present in a Retreat, to make it a Retreat, is not to quarrel over terms. It is to contend for a principle. Seclusion from the familiar scenes and affairs of daily life is strictly essential to the idea of Retreat, because only so can be effectively secured that release from strain which is one of the objects of Retreat. In ordinary surroundings one is inevitably reminded of the things that make Christian life difficult ; strain is suggested ; therefore in Retreat it is necessary that we should get away from them.

In itself, of course, the service of God is by no means a thing of strain. We do not associate the idea of stress with the ministry of angels ; and clearly our Lord would have us keep the calm and peaceful mind ever before us as an ideal even in our service of Him upon earth. The heavy-laden are bidden to come to Him to find rest, and His peace is promised to us as our possession. But here amid things temporal, in the confusions of the world and the weakness of our mortal nature, we do ordinarily find difficulty in the service of God. The soul is ever subject to the sheer drag of the earthly side of things—cares, anxieties, duties, and the unceasing conflict with temptation—pulling against the attractions of the Divine Love. This is true of all of us whatever be our position in life, even though the outward forms and occasions of the disharmony be various.

Now there is nothing more fatal to faculties of any kind than a constant condition of unrelieved stress ; and nothing can revive a faculty so surely as a moment of relief. We grip, let us say, some object with our hand, and endeavour to maintain our grasp. Soon we find that the muscles of the arm lose all power ; we relax, and, after even a short relief, we find that once more we can tighten our hold.

So also for the brain-worker periods of diversion are necessary in order to maintain the power of thinking, and even to pre-

vent a serious breakdown in health.   We
know too (for we are being taught it rather
wonderfully by recent medical discovery)
that the tired mind makes the tired body.
But we seem only just to be discerning
the deeper fact that the tired spirit makes
both ; that neurasthenia is very commonly
the result of spiritual stress ; and that the
contribution that the Church has to make
to the health of the world, to mention for
the moment no higher consideration, is to
show that harmony of spirit is a necessary
condition of full health of mind and body.

But this spiritual vigour cannot be
maintained without periods of relief from
the things that assault and vex the soul.
The disaster of the common neglect of
this truth is by no means perceived yet
as it ought to be.   We can all point, of
course, to clergy and other workers who
are stale and fagged-out ; who are not
only doing no good in their parishes but
are even undoing the good they have done,
because, in a tragic misuse of the sense of
duty, they persist in plodding wearily
along ; keeping machinery in motion,
possibly, but exercising no influence because they are dimmed in faith and bereft
of vision.   Yet that is only a small part

of the trouble. The power of religion is weakened by spiritual weariness in every sphere of modern life. The danger is the same for the business-man as for the priest; for the house-wife and the labourer as it is for the teacher. Probably, as a matter of fact, the chief part of the tragedy is to be found at the present day in a quarter where it is seldom looked for, that is, in the thousands of lads and girls in factory life who give up the practice of religion in despair, because they have never been shown a way of relief from the sickening monotony of facing daily the sheer secularity of modern industry, and that contempt for holy things which is all too common among those whom they are bound to accept as their companions.

Now, if our Lord's witness is to be heeded, we may say confidently that, however constant be the power of temptation or the opportunities of the kingdom, it is not the will of God that the lives of His servants should be spent in unrelieved conflict and labour. Times of withdrawal are the appointed remedy for weariness of soul. Just as a young swimmer may become dispirited through battling with the waves, till he despairs of mastering his art, and then may find confidence restored by bathing one day in a quiet pool ; so souls, finding dryness through the difficulties of life, may recover the joy of the service of God through the calm seclusion of a Retreat. How many a Retreatant has testified to this ! ' I nearly gave up trying ; but now I mean to start again, and I believe I can ' ; this is the sort of expression with which every Conductor is familiar. Consider, too, the revelation of such a phrase as the following, which once came from the lips of a man : ' I used to think my prayers tiresome and impossible. I learned in Retreat that it was my own selfish worrying and haste that wearied me.' But it cannot be insisted upon too plainly that the only seclusion that can bring this relief is one of some duration, and that is completely free from suggestion, through sight or hearing, of the ordinary scenes and occupations of life.

The only practical religion that ' overcometh the world ' is a religion of joy in conflict. At present our organizations, even of the most directly spiritual sort, often fail to produce the effects we look for, largely because we are appealing to the spiritually strained and weary. Give us among our people souls revived by times of stepping aside from the wear and tear of life, and much will be changed. One half of our organizations will stand revealed as unnecessary. The other half will become, not cumbrous machinery, but an effective ordering of power.

CHAPTER IV

THE SILENCE OF RETREAT

MODERN literature, of almost every type between the popular and the recondite, abounds with references to silence as a power of which life at the present day has very special need. Thus, in a recent volume of essays, we read that there is a most important part of a man's being that does not reveal itself in the ordinary ways of life, ' of whose very existence he is only made aware in solitude and silence. And if there happens to be no silence in his life, if he is never solitary, then he may go down to his grave without a knowledge of its existence, much less an understanding of its nature or realization of its potentialities.' [1] Then, turning to literature of another sort, we find an evening paper providing for its readers a series of ' Tonic Talks,' of which not the least interesting is an appeal that times of

[1] *Along the Road*, by Aldous Huxley.

silence should be given a regular place in
life as a sheer necessity for maintaining
calmness, right judgement, and strength
of purpose.

When we consider this we are conscious
of misgivings. Is it not true that here,
in this question of silence, is a matter
wherein the Church is not leading, but
lagging behind, the intelligent thought of
the world ? Secular thinkers of almost
every sort have rediscovered the fact that
silence is golden ; in the outlook and
activities of the Church, almost alone, it
is commonly treated with contempt. Many
of our leaders seem persuaded that nothing can possibly be happening unless we
are talking about it, and contriving organizations for its further discussion ! Some
regard Retreat Houses as tolerable only
because at least they can be used con-
veniently for the purpose of conferences.
The reports of our endless assemblies and
debates have already earned for us a
reputation for being the most talkative
religious body that Christendom has ever
produced, though it is not often alleged
that we are the most effective.

We cannot claim, moreover, that matters are any better in our ordinary parochial

D

life. Parish priests, in their manifold
activities, are required to be of effective
speech and great organizing capacity ;
men of perspiration, in fact, rather than
of aspiration. Most of our methods, too,
seem to be framed on a complete inability
to distinguish between the giving of an
impression and the growth of an idea.
If the former process alone were necessary
for the moving of life then indeed we
should have worked wonders in our time !
For in any busy, active parish, capably
run, the minds of the people are subjected
to a hail-storm of impressions. They are
hurried from one special service to another ;
from sermon to conference ; from debate
to committee meeting ; from this or that
guild or institution to some breathless fête
or function. They hear, they act, perhaps
they read—but are we sure that they are
being helped to think ? Is it not rather
true that many of our Church-folk are
spiritually sick and dizzy ? In the bliz-
zard of impressions they are bewildered.
In the multitude of organizations they do
not know what to do ; in the medley of
opinions they do not know what to believe.
Their minds, more even than those of their
many fellow-victims of modern education

outside the Church, resemble the sand at a sea-side resort just after it has been trodden by the feet of a multitude of excursionists. They have become a wilderness of confused tracks, leading nowhere in particular, and all of which are liable to be wiped out by the rising of the next tide.

The great truth that needs to be made plain in face of all this state of things, and which has especially to be impressed upon those who are making their first Retreat, is that silence is a thing of power. It is not, as is usually supposed, a negative condition of not talking, and therefore unnatural and irksome. It is a positive, creative condition requisite for the due education of some of the deepest faculties we possess, and, in particular, necessary for the sifting of impressions, and the growth of those which are true into ideas clear enough and strong enough to be motive forces in life. It is the almost total neglect of cultivating the discipline of silence among our people that has led to that want of either restraint or effort of thought — that habit of turning away satiated by even a few moments of mental concentration—which even school teachers, to say nothing of the clergy, have learned to dread as one of the greatest hindrances to their work.

Silence, therefore, in Retreat is not the fad of a certain type of Conductor. It is of the essence of Retreat. Even the seclusion which we have been considering is useless without that interior stillness that only silence can secure, and apart from which the practice of Retreat cannot be expected to bring either vision or renewal of motive. The recovery, too, of the treasury of silence, in ordinary devotions apart from Retreat, will prove to be one of the greatest contributions which the Retreat movement is making to the spiritual life of our age.

But, because silence is golden——a thing of great value——it is not to be gained by any who refuse to pay the price. The gift is to be won easily only by a few rare temperaments ; and such will not be found among those who, in the ordinary ways of life, have feared stillness and avoided solitude. On this point the Conductor must be very clear in his explanation ; the price of silence must be paid, by most people at least, in the form of no little difficulty at the start in retaining self-control. There will be for many an hour or two, here and there in the Retreat, that drags. But to say this is, of course, only to state a truth that is evident in the case of every experience or accomplishment that is worth acquiring. The skilled rider did not like his first half-hour in the saddle, nor the strong swimmer his first immersion in the waves. Yet neither of them, in the present enjoyment of his powers, would refuse to pay the price again if it were necessary. Therefore the wise Conductor will fairly warn his Retreatants that, if they hesitate to face the difficulty of a few hours, they will be losing, for perhaps long years afterwards, a priceless possession, and may even be debarring themselves from ever finding a real part of life's true meaning.

It follows that Retreats in which the rule of silence is omitted, or reduced to such an extent that the principle is not retained, are not in fact Retreats ; and what is more, they do not, as so often urged, ' lead people on ' to the desire for a full Retreat. This plea, surely, is an error. For people come into Retreat from a sense of need ; they ' want something,' even though they may have little notion of what it is they seek. Give them a so-called Retreat without the rule of silence, and that need is not met. So far from being attracted towards a further, and possibly more searching, experience, they go away disappointed, feeling that after all there ' is not much in it,' and they have no particular desire to enter a Retreat House again. On the other hand if the silence be strictly kept, even with difficulty, the need is met. They go away satisfied, and desire in due course to come into Retreat again. So then any advocate who seeks to gain Retreatants by representing the experience in a false light, and belittling the demand of silence, courts nothing less than the danger of turning souls aside from the way. A Retreat is a simple thing ; it is just, as we have seen, a special visit that we pay to God. But no one has any right to attempt to make it easy, for in nothing is it more true than that we receive in the measure that we bring.

Let a final plea be added for weighing the principle that is at stake. A Church that carries on activities apart from the background of silence will lose its power in an endless shifting of methods that lack motives, till the Nemesis of despondency chills its very life. The Christian soul that looks for satisfaction in hearing and doing, but never in still waiting and silent thinking, will empty itself of every power that really matters, in an endless seeking that never becomes a finding.

Let a Retreat therefore be a Retreat, and nothing else, that it may bring its own special gifts of realization. We have plenty of room in our Church's life as well for all the conferences and social gatherings we may need. Silence is too precious, too subtle, and too bitterly needed by us to be tampered with when we go apart from the world.

CHAPTER V

THE EFFECTS OF RETREAT

THE Retreat is often regarded with some measure of suspicion as though it were, so to speak, a backwater of the spiritual life rather than a current in its main stream. Diocesan committees, for instance, express yearnings for a Retreat House, as for something that would be a most desirable possession if only circumstances permitted the Church to consider amenities as well as necessities. Clergy, too, will sometimes be found who hesitate to urge their people to go into Retreat from a sort of undefined misgiving, lest, having made trial of the practice, they should acquire a hankering for eccentric ways of devotion, that make them discontented with the ordinary means of grace to be found in their parish church. It is, indeed, this fear that will often be found to explain the stubborn, yet unformulated, opposition that sometimes proceeds from the clergy against any vigorous and definite movement for the extension of Retreat. It is interpreted as a criticism of the normal methods they employ.

If only this illusion could be banished, and the real truth grasped, the progress of the Retreat movement would be finally assured. For the characteristic effect of Retreat is to induce not discontent, but a deeper appreciation of all the ordinary spiritual privileges that the clergy offer to their people. Retreat may indeed make them more discriminating ; stones will not be so easily accepted in place of bread. But if in fact bread is being offered in any given parish, then there is nothing to compare with the Retreat for making people realize its true nature and their own real needs.

' I used to go to church fairly often, and I cannot say it meant very much to me. Since my Retreat I have gone whenever I can, and I have discovered meanings in every service that I never knew were there.' This sentence, spoken by a busy woman in whose life religion had been likely to die, is typical of a wide volume of testimony. The importance of it is to show that the Retreat does not constitute a criticism of parochial methods, neither is it offered as a substitute for them. On the contrary, it reinforces all that a faithful priest normally does for his people in spirit and in truth. Thus, since we cannot but admit that much of the labour which the clergy to-day find irksome is not strictly a part of their spiritual ministrations, but is forced upon them by reason of prevalent ignorance and apathy, the Retreat goes wonderfully far to lighten their burden. It removes much of the causes of the difficulty and dryness of their work by bringing their flock to a better understanding of the pastoral object of a parish priest. ' I used to think,' said one who had learned the truth by experience, ' that I had far too much to do already to dream of getting my people into Retreat. I know now that nothing in the world has ever before saved me so much trouble.' Said another, ' Ever since their Retreat my people have been so much easier to lead ! I feel now that I have their sympathy in all I am trying to do.'

How this sort of result is brought about can be readily shown by witness from the other side. The leader of a group of laymen once said to a Conductor, as they parted, ' We are going back really to help the vicar now. At last we see what he is out for.' ' I've been a churchwarden for fifteen years,' said a companion, ' and now I begin to see what it really means to be a Churchman.' If only this one typical result of Retreat could be made more widely known among clergy, the mere yearning for houses of Retreat would disappear. There would rise in its place an insistent demand, led by the clergy themselves, that houses should be provided on a sufficient scale throughout the land.

Again, out of this quickened understanding of the meaning of the life of faith (which is in itself simply the revived sense of joy in the Lord that Retreat so powerfully brings) there grows, in some cases very remarkably, a new spirit of consecration.

Strenuous are our attempts nowadays to induce people to serve ; yet many of them fail because, so often, they amount to nothing but the organizing and reorganizing of comparative apathy. The Retreat succeeds because, deepening the soul's sense of its indebtedness to the Saviour, a right motive is established. The point is worth dwelling upon, because it concerns so very much of the problems of our time. There has possibly never been an age so full as ours of vigorous endeavour, directed expressly towards the betterment of human life. Yet it is difficult to resist the conclusion that equally in our educational, social, and religious work we have reaped much failure because we have been so anxiously concerned with the provision of ways and means, methods and machinery, and have paid so little attention to the more essential object of renewing motives. Thus so much of our efforts (and the stricture applies not least to common parochial methods) has resembled the building of costly, elaborate, cumbrous staircases for the benefit of people who do not particularly wish to ascend.

Thus, in the particular matter we are considering, the Church's call to serve is more and more insistently sounded ; opportunities of service are anxiously provided ; and yet the kingdom of God is delayed for want of a compelling motive for consecration. The remedy is not the provision of more staircases, regardless of labour and cost, till the backs of the clergy are finally broken by the strain of supporting them. On the contrary, if a man wants to go upstairs the elaborate staircase is not really required ; any rough ladder that comes to hand will do. So, if we could but quicken one little bit the spiritual motive of our people, the first result would be an immense simplifying of our organization. It is not keen people, but only the half-hearted, who need incessant arranging and oversight of the ways and means of the work they are carrying on.

Now it is just this quickening of the motive to serve that is one of the most astonishing results of Retreat, especially in the case of young people. Again and again groups of Retreatants have gone back into their parishes, and have proceeded to do things, to the surprise and joy of the clergy, that they would never have dreamed of doing if they had not been brought to the experience of Retreat. Sometimes these have been simple things requiring no organizing, but only willingness and common sense. Sometimes they have been sustained efforts, requiring rather more in the way of supervision. But in all cases the mark has been spontaneous initiative rather than a grudging response to appeal. ' My boys,' said a vicar, ' have been a perfect nuisance ever since their Retreat. They are perpetually wanting something more to do.' A heaped up measure of that particular sort of nuisance would transform the Church of England, and remove from us one of the particular reproaches levelled at us now by the new Churches of the Dominions !

But, of course, beyond this immediate impulse to do something at once in the parish, there lies the deeper question of vocation. No one with much experience as a Conductor will fail to testify to the effects of Retreat in this respect. Our missionary councils, indeed, are declaring that the response to the mission call will depend largely on the spread of Retreats in the immediate future. Again, if our youths and young men of to-day were going into Retreat generally, instead of exceptionally, a generation would arise forthwith in which the shortage of candidates for the ministry would cease to be a formidable menace.

Finally, though this perhaps may prove to be the most important effect of all, the Retreat creates, as does nothing else in our methods, the sense of apostleship. At the present moment, though it is claimed that there is a reviving interest in religion, there is in fact no endeavour of the Church that seems so little fruitful as that of actual reconversion. The atmosphere of a diocesan evangelistic council is usually one of hesitation and doubt. Missions of various kinds are tried ; they make a stir, and are certainly appreciated by religious folk ; but no means at our present disposal seem to have the power of lifting men from the pavement into the Church.

But may it not be that we have been looking for the secret of success in a wholly wrong direction ? Is it not the real truth that the Church has so little converting power because it has so few members with a sense of apostleship ? There is in the world to-day a prevalent attitude towards religion which, let it be admitted at once, has gravely and widely affected our Church people's outlook, and which is incompatible with the spirit of evangelism. It is to regard religion, among many other things, as a matter of quite admissible personal taste. One man is musical and plays the fiddle ; another is scientific and collects butterflies ; a third is religious and goes to church. No one wishes to quarrel with any of the three, nor expects himself to be disturbed! The result is, we have a large number of Church members, who personally value their religion highly. They would make the stubbornest of martyrs if any one sought to deprive them of it. But of an energetic sense of apostleship they have hardly a trace.

We are often told from platforms that we are on the eve of a great revival ; that we must do this or that in order to reap the opportunity. But history shows quite conclusively that a great age of conversion has never come about under official direction. The Church has never advanced, in this or any other way, by roads authoritatively engineered and pontifically declared open. Revival has always come, after an age of dryness, by the spurting out of spiritual energy from unforeseen quarters, and not seldom, indeed, in unauthorized ways. The saying may be trite, but it is true, that religion must be caught before it can be taught. It is not, therefore, by devising ever fresh means of bringing people in the mass within range of accredited missioners' voices that very much gain is to be hoped for—none at all indeed if that is to stand alone. Wider conversion will come only by deepening in the Church such a spirit as will produce prophets and apostles among the people themselves.

There are signs, perhaps, though not very distinct yet, of the revival of the spirit of prophecy. But it is clear and certain that the Retreat is awakening, in ordinary people, the sense of apostleship. It is as yet a small rift, but yet a real breaking of the clouds, and, as far as one can see, the only one. Not only have individual Retreatants been known to experience a deep change of mind on the whole matter, and have forthwith influenced others as they have never attempted to before ; but, what is even more significant, groups of Retreatants have in not a few cases banded themselves together for some definite evangelistic object, and have carried out works as the result of Retreat that show what might come to pass if Retreatants were the many instead of the few in our religious life.

The Retreat House, difficult to create, costly to maintain, and ministering only to small groups of people, seems still to many to be an extravagance hard to justify in our mission work. It is indeed

E

significant that very little attention has been paid, even by those in authority, to the fact that the Archbishops' Committee of 1916 on Home Mission Work declared a Retreat House to be among the first necessities of a diocesan missionary organization. The truth is that the holding of a Retreat impresses the ordinary imagination so much less than the crowded service for men, the prosperous club for lads, or the well-advertized mission that for a time was the talk of a town. But if the contention be true that it is the Retreat, far more than the other means, that really sets free the enthusiasm of apostleship among the people themselves, that alone decides which is the surest way to the reconversion of our nation.

CHAPTER VI

RETREATANTS

THE introduction of the formal Retreat into the life of the Church of England took place shortly after the middle of last century, and, as is well known, the credit is due to some of the most honoured names among the leaders of the Oxford Movement.[1] But it is unfortunately true that from that beginning, until about ten years ago, very little progress was made. Much the same number of people, clergy and laity, went into Retreat year by year, and that number was far too small to have any wide or obvious influence upon the Church's life as a whole.

There is nothing mysterious about the reason for this stagnation. There was but a limited vision of what could be achieved by means of Retreat, and in consequence

---

[1] For a fuller treatment of the historical aspect the reader is referred to a chapter by the present writer in *Retreats* (S.P.C.K., 1927).

a disregard of the methods necessary for its wider extension. It was assumed, if not quite universally yet by all but a very few, that the Retreat was suited to people of a restricted type ; only, in fact, clergy and the more experienced laity of a certain devotional tendency. Retreats were therefore seldom arranged except by some diocesan official, or the authorities of a community house. They formed a little enclosed corner of the Church's spiritual endeavour which parish priests, even when sympathetically inclined, did not regard as having anything to do with their own normal ministry to the rank and file of their people.

It is in this respect that we have been brought to a great discovery that is being justified now by a growing experience every year. We know that we can no longer mark off certain sorts of people as being ' fit for Retreat ' or ' ready for Retreat.' One cannot doubt that here lay, in the last generation, one of the many evil results of ' intellectualism,' that is to say, of that long-inherited tendency to treat the rational understanding as if it were almost the only faculty worth considering in spiritual training. But now from practically every Retreat House in the land the Church is being re-taught the simple lesson of the equality of souls. Want of religious knowledge is not at all the same thing as lack of spiritual capacity. Man is by nature a spiritual being ; normally, and not through the accident of having been instructed, he has within him the power of realizing the spiritual and laying hold upon God. It is the Church's function to train, but not to create, this power ; and seclusion and silence are priceless aids to its emergence at any stage of its development. There is only one qualification required of a Retreatant. It is indeed an indispensable one, but it does not consist of long experience or much instruction. It is a simple Godward intention. Let that be present and any human soul may find help, or possibly the crisis of a lifetime, through the experience of Retreat. Again and again it has been shown that the very people whom parish priests hesitate to send into Retreat, as being too simple or too little experienced, are those who are most likely to become grounded and settled by the venture.

On reconsidering the matter, in the

light of experience and, we may say, a
better knowledge of human nature than
our immediate forefathers seem to have
possessed, there is nothing surprising in
the fact of this wider application of the
Retreat method, which is taking place
before our eyes so wonderfully that it is
being called the most hopeful spiritual
movement of our age.

In the first place it should surely be
recognized that what was attested so
plainly in our Lord's own Perfect Manhood, in His life upon earth, was not
likely to have been intended as a privilege
for a select few, but rather as a principle
for humanity—a way of experience for
man as man.

Then, again, it is obvious that the
immediate purpose of Retreat is, by its
seclusion and silence, to render easier the
activity of spiritual powers, through re-
moval of the hindrances met with in
ordinary life. It would seem, then, to
follow logically that it is the inexperi-
enced, rather than the adept, who stand
most in need of this assistance. If a
mother is wise in choosing the smoothest
path for her baby's earliest steps ; if a
hospital nurse does well to remove chairs

and mats out of the way of a patient recovering the use of his limbs, then surely (if we must discriminate between various types) the method of Retreat is likely to be of most help to those who have made little progress in the art of the spiritual life. In any case, apart from theory, it is unquestionably among adolescents, and those mostly of the less educated classes, that the Retreat is doing its widest work at the present time. It cannot, also, be too clearly understood that it is proving to be deeply effective among many of this class whom other more popular methods have signally failed to impress.

At this point a word should be said about Retreats for children, though this is so specialized a branch of the work as to require a handbook to itself for adequate treatment.

Some people who have never witnessed a Retreat for young children seem disposed to combine their preconceived notions of Retreats and of children, and so to picture to themselves a most undesirable proceeding. They imagine the young folk induced by some strange magic to listen to long and numerous exhortations, and going out from so doleful an occasion confirmed little prigs for the rest of their lives. In passing it may be mentioned that here one can detect again the trail of ' intellectualism '—in the idea that there is something ' unnatural ' and ' aping the grown-up ' in the use by children of spiritual faculties, before they can be expected to have ' learned to understand ' their religion. We shall surely never make much headway in the training of the young except by methods that embody a full recognition of the fact that they are, as truly as their elders, spiritual beings.

But, to avoid going too far into somewhat profound questions, we would simply urge that the objectors are much in the position of the professor who evolved a camel out of his own inner consciousness, and disdained the advice of his friends to go to the menagerie and see the beast in real life ! Children, in the testimony of all those who have qualified themselves to judge by experience, make excellent Retreatants. Once more the reason is quite clear ; it is that simplicity is a mark of child nature. The spiritual faculties of a child respond to the favourable conditions of Retreat more spontaneously than those of an adult person, and emerge naturally and happily in worship, prayer, and thanksgiving, without any of that emotional strain which sometimes produces a suggestion of unreality in the Retreats of their elders.

There is, too, a special reason which explains why the results of Retreat are often so long-enduring in children's lives and outlook, and why parish priests who have once sent Confirmation candidates into Retreat (if only they be young enough —for the elder ' teens ' are a much less satisfactory age) are always anxious to include Retreat afterwards as a normal part of their preparation. It concerns that whole great question of what the psychologists call ' the initial impulse.' In the past our educational endeavours have proceeded largely upon the assumption that two things only are necessary to ensure habits of any sort, but especially of devotion. These are a steady training in the routine of those habits, and a careful explanation of their object and value. This notion has long held sway among us, and is still widely clung to, fitting in as it does with the peculiar temperament of the typically Anglican mind. It has become, nevertheless, an idol, and we ought not to be sorry to see the conditions of our times, and a sounder psychology, smashing it to pieces before our eyes. The real truth is that routine and instruction are very far from being the only factors in the matter, or even the main ones. There is no life in which the importance of a strong initial impulse is negligible in the forming of a habit ; and in most lives, of the ordinary sort with which we have to deal, it is the dominant factor. In the majority of cases a vivid early impression and a short training will hold, whereas a long training and a monotony of slight impressions will merely let slip. Those who seek to remedy the leakage from the Church after Confirmation *only* by a longer training before it, are basing their reform upon a discredited view of human nature. We lose the young, not merely because we have not trained them, but far more because we have not, with any violence, impressed them.

Now it is this ' initial impulse,' this vivid impression, that the Retreat provides, as nothing else does that we have discovered yet for children. The stillness and solemnity of Retreat, the reality and joyfulness, the quiet energy and silent fellowship, all these and other elements combine to leave a very deep mark upon the minds of the young, and especially to suggest an association of religion with happiness. And this impression is of value chiefly for the reason that it is imparted in the earlier stages of spiritual experience, instead of being deferred till life is too complicated, and often too unnatural, easily to receive any impression of truth at all.

The Retreat House, then, is opening its doors now, and must do so even more widely in future, to all sorts and conditions of people. Conductors, therefore, must be prepared to face, not only a few types who may be expected to share their own outlook, experience, and phraseology; but, at different times, the young and the old, the lettered and the unlettered, the devout and the seekers, the thoughtful and those who have little control of their mental processes—all in fact of every kind who know that they want God. And to grasp this marvellous opportunity we must face what will probably be a long period of the learning of manifold applications of the great principles of Retreat.

But, it may be asked, how are all these various people to be brought into Retreat ?

The answer is, by means of the Parochial Retreat. In the past, because the true scope and possibilities of Retreats were unrecognized, there was contentment with a very defective method of arranging them. As a rule a Retreat was organized by a diocesan missioner, or some official remote from ordinary members of a congregation, and the clergy were merely asked to give out a notice calling attention to it. This they did—generally in conjunction with, perhaps, a dozen other notices dealing with more familiar matters ! It is hardly too much to say that, in the present state of popular understanding of the meaning of Retreat, they might as well have given out notice of a pogrom or a corroboree for all that it conveyed to the majority of their people ! From here and there were attracted a few, who already knew the value of Retreat. They attended, and afterwards were scattered to the four quarters of their diocese, so that the force of their witness was largely lost.

Retreats thus centrally arranged have, doubtless, value in themselves as much as any other sort of Retreat. They will always, too, be rightly appreciated by busy Church-workers who need in their

Retreat separation from the people among whom they work. The service rendered by our Community Houses is, even for this reason alone, of incalculable value. But the main way of advance is undoubtedly along the line of the Parochial Retreat. The date of this is arranged with the authorities of the Retreat House by the parish priest, and, if he does not intend to conduct the Retreat himself, a suitable conductor is secured by him. The whole matter then rests, as it rightly should, with him and his colleagues in the parish. It is for them to teach their people about Retreat ; to form the Retreat party, taking as much care as possible, not necessarily to separate sexes, for ' mixed Retreats ' have a special value; [1] but to secure homogeneity as to age and especially experience, for beginners require different treatment from those who have been into Retreat

[1] *The value of ' mixed' Retreats.* It is significant that hardly any problem can be discussed for very long without working back to that question of ' home religion,' which lies at the root of nearly all of them. Now, by common admission, the cause of the weakness is to be found in the fact that, even when the members of a household are severally religious, there is very little atmosphere, or sharing, of religion in the home. Religion is only exceptionally the realized common

before. It is for the parish priests, in
short, to set forth the Retreat as a privilege
offered in their own ministry to their own
people, and to do all they can adequately
to prepare for Retreat those whom they
have encouraged to go. Thus the Retreat
is made to appear as a normal, rather than
merely extraordinary, event ; and, what
matters most of all, when the Retreat is
over the group comes back into the life
and work of the parish with all the explo-
sive force of witness and enthusiasm that
can only come from people who together
have shared a corporate vision.

This is the answer to the objection, not
seldom heard, ' My people want not stillness but an earthquake.' It is the cease-
less round of activities that becomes flat ;
it is the withdrawal into quiet that revives
power. It is when this simple truth is
testified to among ordinary people by their
fellows, with an enthusiasm that is its own
assurance of truth, that the life of a parish
begins to be shaken with a new energy.

bond of family life. The practice of husbands and
wives, sisters and brothers, fathers and daughters going
through the experience of Retreat together is a sovereign remedy. ' Thank God for this,' said a man on
leaving Retreat ; ' now my wife and I can talk together
about spiritual things.'

PART TWO

THE CONDUCTING OF RETREATS

CHAPTER I

THE MAIN PRINCIPLES

NOTHING can be expressed more simply than the secret of the art of conducting Retreats. It is to be found in remembering that the very word Conductor means one who leads, and not one who merely speaks. Ample allowance must, of course, be made in this, as in any other ministration, for personal temperament and gifts. But it can safely be said that no methods of conducting Retreats can possibly be sound that are not based all through upon this plain fact.

It must, however, be admitted that, though this first principle when thus briefly stated may seem clear and incontrovertible, it has not been by any means universally followed in practice. We have indeed inherited from the past generation a tradition of conducting so faulty that the usefulness of Retreat is often very seriously diminished. By an ignoring of the true technique of the art of conducting, as well as through some confusion of idea as to the proper object of Retreat, the addresses have come to loom far too large in the minds of priests and people alike. Thus Retreats frequently amount to little more than the delivery of a series of sermons, indistinguishable as regards subject from any devotional course that might be preached in a church. Some quite arbitrarily selected religious theme, or passage of Holy Scripture, is expounded to the hearers after various irrelevant services, spaced out over two or three days of a silence that is but little profitable by reason of its purpose not being clearly understood.

This has brought about two very unfortunate results, both of which are real hindrances to the extension of the practice of Retreat. In the first place, many people have found no particular benefit in Retreat ; they do not see why they should have been put to the expense and trouble of going to a distant house in order to listen to discourses, which were no doubt excellent in their way, but might have been equally well delivered in their own parish church. Again, positive discredit has been brought upon the Retreat movement by the spectacle of other people of a certain type, claiming to be enthusiasts for the cause, and yet understanding its purpose so little that they refuse to go to any Retreat at all unless it is taken by ' Father Blank, who gives such beautiful addresses.'

A priest, then, who undertakes the work of conducting must set out from the realization that his business is not essentially either exposition or exhortation. What is required of him is to evoke the spiritual faculties of the Retreatants, and to assist and guide them in the transactions that take place between themselves and God. He is not equipped for his task by reason of having prepared certain discourses, even if he possesses the necessary skill for delivering them acceptably. He need say nothing—indeed he should say nothing — except what is strictly necessary to help his hearers along an ordered course of spiritual exercises, having for their object a clearer realization of the will of God for the particular lives of those present, and the due reordering of those lives to be more in harmony with that will. Too much elaboration of doctrine, still more of exhortation, can be a very real hindrance in Retreat. Indeed a Retreat may be perfectly valid and extremely fruitful, though it lacks altogether the presence of a Conductor—at least in the sense of one who gives addresses. This is proved by the increasing number of people who year by year derive great benefit from the practice of solitary Retreat, and find all the assistance that they need in the Sacrament of the Altar, a devotional book or two, and a little guidance from some experienced priest.

On the other hand it must not be supposed from what has just been said that, in a conducted Retreat, the addresses are unimportant. On the contrary, they largely determine the spiritual result of the whole undertaking, since all first Retreatants, and the great majority of the more experienced, are to a large extent dependent upon them for a fruitful use of the time. But what is meant, in all that has been written thus far, is that the addresses must be strictly relevant to the main object in hand. They should not be disconnected from each other ; still less should they be, as a whole, remote from the purpose of Retreat which, it cannot be insisted upon too often, is realization rather than learning. No Conductor should go to a Retreat, as he might go to preach in a church, satisfied if his proposed sermon is lucid and generally suited to an average congregation. He must be at pains to ascertain the precise sort of people he is called upon to deal with, not only in regard to sex or age or even educational attainment, but still more in respect of their religious outlook and level of spiritual experience. He must then draw up a plan of Retreat, roughly expressed in his time-table but destined to be particularly developed in his addresses, which he thinks is the most likely to help those particular people to come to a closer walk with God. This plan should be articulated into definite stages, and each address, and for that matter each service too, should be strictly intended to elucidate the particular stage in hand at any given moment. If the Conductor forsakes this aim of leading his Retreatants along a definite path of realization, mainly by the use of their own faculties, and descends to the lower and much easier occupation of retaining their interest by attractive preaching, he will no doubt receive thanks from more than one for his helpful addresses. But in the true work of a Conductor he will reap sad failure.

A word should be said here concerning 'Ignatian Retreats.' A good deal of confusion has been introduced into this question through the phrase being used in more than one sense. Strictly speaking an 'Ignatian Retreat' ought to mean a Retreat in which full employment is made of the 'Ignatian method.' But it can hardly be claimed that any Retreat of less than nine days duration at the least can be 'Ignatian' in this sense. To discuss what this method is, and what it implies, would take us far beyond the scope of this present book.[1] But, perhaps, there are some Conductors who need reminding that a short Retreat of two or three days is not rendered 'Ignatian' by the use of mediaeval Spanish phrases and ideas to express spiritual truths. *Cucullus non facit monachum.* There is, no doubt, a great work to be done among us in the future by the 'Ignatian method,' as people seem to be gradually learning to devote more

[1] Readers are referred to such well-known books as Father Longridge's or Father Rickaby's.

time to their Retreats. But it can be done only by those Conductors who are willing to give such a prolonged study to their subject as to be able thoroughly to adapt Ignatian methods to meet the actual needs and outlook of English people of the present day. There remain, however, two other senses in which, in the opinion, at least, of many besides the present writer, nearly all Retreats, short or long, ought to be Ignatian.

First, in the sense that a Retreat should consist essentially of guided spiritual exercises, and not simply of religious instruction. This point has already been so strongly emphasized in these pages that it is unnecessary further to dwell upon it.

Secondly, a Retreat, however short, should be Ignatian in the sense of following in the main the well-marked stages of the sequence of ideas in the *Spiritual Exercises*. This, let the reader be reminded, is a matter of opinion ; but the fact seems plain that few Conductors of experience, who have also made a study of the Exercises, will be found not to hold the opinion strongly. S. Ignatius has laid down a line of meditation by which the soul can be brought to a sort of Pisgah vision of the meaning of Christian life as a whole, which is far more effective than arbitrarily chosen treatments of restricted phases of truth. It is a line that is capable of such infinite variety of presentation that no monotony need be incurred however often it is undertaken. Seldom anything but loss results from not following in this respect the guidance of him who may rightly be called the founder of the formal Retreat.

It is possible to express shortly the main outline of this sequence of ideas. Beginning from what is called the ' Foundation,' the Retreatant is brought to see that life has meaning and purpose only if God is realized in all things as its object. The soul is thus delivered at the beginning out of the snare of ' departmental ' religion ; the supposition that God is the most important among other of life's objects. It is compelled to face the fact that life is for God alone; that in all things He is the only object, and that the whole purpose of life is lost in everything if this truth be allowed to grow dim. The necessary condition of this realization is shown to be that true ' detachment,' which signifies not aloofness or remoteness from

this world's affairs, but eternal purpose in
the use of all temporal things ; and the
misuse of ' creatures,' i.e. divinely created
faculties and opportunities as well as
things, is declared to be the criterion of
sinfulness. This stage closes with the
solemn consideration of the possibility,
through failure in detachment, of aliena-
tion from God, and eternal loss.

Secondly, the soul thus finding God
as life's only object, is not led to the
discovery of some abstract philosophy of
life, but is confronted with the personal and
searching call of the kingdom. Christ's
throne is the centre of this, and definite
choice must be made to serve either under
the standard of Mount Sion or the standard set up over the plains of Babylon.
Here the Conductor will dwell, in any one
of the hundred ways that are possible,
on the glory of our Lord's kingdom and
the falseness of the allurements of the
world, the flesh, and the devil.

Thirdly, the Cross is held up before the
Retreatant's eyes. He is brought to
understand, not that it represents the cruel
death of a great Teacher, or a mere symbol
of self-denial, but that Jesus Christ, Who
has been worshipped upon His throne of

glory, is the same Lord Who gave His all-holy life on Calvary, that the kingdom might be won, and the gates of redemption opened. Here, of necessity, comes in the consideration of the Penitential Life which is the soul's response to the call of the Passion. In his guidance at this stage perhaps the greatest responsibility, as well as opportunity, is presented to the Conductor.

Finally, the fourth stage is devoted to the realization of the Unitive Way. The details, no doubt of set purpose, are not filled in by S. Ignatius' own hand ; but clearly the Conductor should seek to end his task for the Retreatants by bringing them to as vivid a realization as possible of the meaning of the life of grace.

Conductors, therefore, even if they have no intention of becoming exponents of the whole Ignatian method (for the operation of which, indeed, but few opportunities are as yet provided), should nevertheless give a close and prolonged study to the Ignatian Exercises. At first they may find them puzzling and difficult ; but they will be rewarded, as the underlying principles become clear, by gaining a grip upon the real nature and purpose of

Retreat such as they can hardly hope to secure in any other way. If this were to become more general there would follow the avoidance of much of the ineffectiveness and waste of opportunity, that are present to-day in many Retreats, which get souls no further than a mild sensation of restfulness and pleasant, but not very searching, instruction.

CHAPTER II

SOME PARTICULAR CONSIDERATIONS

PENITENCE ; RULES OF LIFE

MUCH of the absence of joy and lack of satisfaction, that is more or less characteristic of modern religion, in such strong contrast to the religion of the New Testament, is without question the result of too shallow an experience of the penitential life. For penitence, in spite of the apparent tenor of a certain type of Lenten address, is not its own object. We are not called to penitence for its own sake, nor in order to rest therein. Repentance of sin is required of the soul as the condition of realizing the joy of life reconciled with God in Christ. Since, therefore, the effect of making a good Retreat is a more vivid apprehension of the meaning of the Unitive Way, it follows that any Retreat must come short of its

object which does not impart in some
measure the capacity for a deeper penitence.

It has already been suggested that
herein lies the responsibility which the
Conductor is likely to feel most keenly
of all. If he is worthy of his work he will
scorn to be the minister of the spurious
and transient elation which can be brought
about by merely attractive speaking. He
will know that there can be no increase
of real and abiding joy in the Retreatants'
lives except in the measure that, under
his guidance, they have been led into a
deeper conviction of sin, and a clearer
apprehension of how they may rid themselves of its burden.

Yet here again it must be admitted that
we are suffering from an unwise and
cramping tradition. For there has been
in the past a widespread tendency among
Conductors to assume that effectiveness in
this part of their endeavours should of
necessity show itself in the greatest possible number of immediate confessions. Consequently an idea is common among priests
and people that Retreat is inevitably
associated with the making of confession.

There are certainly not a few among the

experienced Conductors of to-day who are gravely questioning the wisdom of this method. Most, indeed, would probably be found to hold definitely that it is only a long Retreat—say of a week at least—that is really a suitable occasion for actual confession. If people come to shorter Retreats willing and prepared for the Sacrament of Penance, then the fact should be declared and the rite administered as soon as possible. Sometimes it may be advisable that persons should be encouraged to wait after Retreat, in order to prepare for and make their confessions before leaving the House. It goes, too, without saying that special measures should be taken to meet exceptional cases in which sin of a mortal kind is clearly involved. But, generally speaking and as a matter of principle, the notion that confession is practically a necessary part of any Retreat needs breaking down. The Conductor's true aim is to bring about a clearer conviction of sin ; and if he appears to insist upon this showing itself at once he may be actually defeating his own object. He may easily uproot a seed that has just begun to germinate. The more vivid sense, that he has perhaps awakened, may be checked at once instead of being allowed to develop, if an immediate account be exacted. Furthermore, it is certainly true of many Retreatants, particularly young ones in a short Retreat, that, if they suppose that confession is required of them before they leave, they will become so oppressed and burdened with the business of detailed self-examination as to be prevented from entering profitably into other stages of realization. Thus the chief results of the Retreat as a whole may be altogether lost.

But to plead for thought and discrimination in this matter, rather than the blind following of a tradition, is in no way to lighten the Conductor's burden. It is his bounden duty to afford all the help he can in his addresses, and even more in the private interviews that he should encourage the Retreatants to seek, to ensure that after the Retreat penitence may be deeper, self-examination more fruitful, and confession more real. No one who has experienced Retreat should be content thereafter with a repentance that only looks backward with sorrow rather than forward with resolve ; with a self-examination that discovers only wrong actions rather than sinful motives ; or with a confession that is only the fulfilment of a duty rather than a quest, by the way of the Cross, to recover the joy and power of the Risen Life.

Again, no plan of Retreat can be satisfactory that omits the question of the framing or reordering of rules of life. It may be that the Conductor does not see his way, in a short Retreat, to include in his addresses a full treatment of this subject ; yet even so he should refer to it in such a way as to encourage the Retreatants to seek his help in private guidance. He will find, too, that it is assistance of this sort that is most often required of him in interviews.

In offering such assistance it is indeed well to remember the old saying of a French doctor: ' Il n'y a pas des maladies, mais il y a beaucoup des malades.' Advice, in other words, must be applicable to persons, not merely to abstract cases. Yet for the majority of people there are two governing principles that need especially to be made clear.

The first depends upon the truth, so often obscured by the exaggerated English fear of formalism, that *forms are formative*. Rules of life are necessary, not at all because we acquire merit by the keeping of them, but because through rules right habits of life can be established. Much that people suppose to be natural or instinctive in their conduct is in reality the direct outcome of early training by rule. We brush our hair, for instance, every morning not because of an inborn tendency to do so, but because our parents made a rule about it and insisted upon its being kept. We sometimes talk too loosely about 'sowing a habit, and reaping a character.' Habits are not sown ; they are formed, and that largely by rule. Consequently the reason why many people's religious habits leave much to be desired is not seldom that there has been remissness concerning the rules by which they might have been established.

Warning, on the other hand, is required by some concerning the danger of regarding rules as the guarantee of spiritual progress. It is only too possible for souls, concentrating on the endeavour to keep rules almost as if that were the whole purpose of the religious life — perhaps dully persisting in some systematic regulation that has long ceased to be helpful— wellnigh to lose all that sense of privi-

G

lege which is a necessary condition for growing sainthood at any of its stages. The Christian vision of God the Father, wanting His children so to order their lives as to become by grace more truly His, sinks into obscurity behind the image of the hard Taskmaster demanding of His servants the daily toll of devotional bricks. No priest who has heard many confessions will deny the gravity of this danger.

Therefore, to such, warning should be given that their rules of life should represent not the maximum of possible attainment, but the minimum below which they will not allow themselves to slip even in the hard and difficult times. Rules should be, as it were, the hand-rail, rather than the staircase, of the soul's ascent. In health a light touch on the rail is sufficient; in weakness it is there as a support lest faintness should lead to a fall. In other words, the sense of obligation should be relied on as a safeguard against apathy and drift ; but it must not be allowed, as one fears it often is, to crush out the higher, yet inclusive, sense of joy in holy endeavour in life and service. Thus, to sum it all up, some Retreatants will be found who are the victims of instability and retarded development through never having perceived, and wisely met, the need of definite rules. Others, hardly less numerous, have suffered loss through an earnest but misdirected use of the same means.

It is the Conductor's task, requiring much insight and particular discrimination, to help both these classes of souls in their difficulties. But this brings us to what is perhaps his own chief need in preparing himself for his work. This is a far fuller knowledge than most priests at present possess of ' ascetic ' theology— the science, that is to say, of the training of the spiritual faculties. It is, when we consider it, rather a strange thing, but undoubtedly true, that the clergy of to-day are more skilled in setting forth world-problems than in solving any personal ones ! It would be easy enough to find in any town preachers who can deal ably and forcibly with such wide subjects as ' Evolution and the doctrine of the Fall,' or ' Prayer in the light of modern psychology.' It would not be so easy, one fears, to find in the same body of men teachers who can effectively show an individual the practical steps to be taken in order to triumph over a given temptation, or to overcome some specific hindrance in his life of prayer. The weakness is, perhaps, being remedied in the training of our younger men. But a far wider realization of this special function of the priestly office is required yet before our Retreats can be as effective as they might be in the strengthening and refreshing of souls.

CHAPTER III

SOME FURTHER CONSIDERATIONS

Intercession ; Resolutions ; Thanksgiving

IT is frankly a matter of dispute among Conductors as to whether intercessions should form part of a Retreat at all.

There are some who argue that a Retreat is essentially a time for withdrawal ; a meeting of the soul alone with God. Intercessions therefore are held to be an intrusion, certain by their very nature to be the occasion of worry and distraction.

Against this contention weighty arguments can be urged from the other side. In the first place personality does not mean isolated individuality, as the above reasoning would seem to imply. What we are, and are becoming, in ourselves, is largely determined by our attitude to others, which is both expressed and rightly developed by intercession. To come into God's presence divested of this attitude would, even if it were possible, mean that we should come not more truly ourselves but maimed. And if people make their relation to others an occasion of worry they should be taught in Retreat to consecrate rather than ignore it.

Then again, intercession is a great way of realizing the meaning of the kingdom, which is one main object of Retreat. This is particularly true of young people, for a reason that will be shown later ; but indeed it may be said of most people that they are more likely to realize fresh truths of the kingdom through well-guided intercessions for its coming into various spheres of their own experience, than through any amount of explanation of its abstract nature.

Thus it may be urged that intercession should certainly not be excluded from the exercises of Retreat, and that this applies particularly to Retreats for beginners. But there should be a definite time allotted for preparation, and not merely a casual request for the putting of subjects into the Conductor's box. Great care, too, should

be bestowed upon conducting an intercession service intelligibly and sympathetically ; for a Retreat should always be a
school for souls, and by the intercessions
of a Retreat many may learn the better to
intercede.

Past practice has, one cannot help
thinking, inclined Conductors as well as
Missioners to undue haste in the encour-
aging of resolutions. They are dangerous
instruments because of that unconscious
counter-suggestion that has already been
touched upon in another connection. ' I
determine to do a thing ' *may* mean that in
reality I am only very strongly emphasiz-
ing its difficulty and thereby destroying
my own confidence. Then again, resolutions that are general, rather than particular, are at all costs to be avoided. They
are rarely anything else than a waste-outlet
for spiritual emotion.

It would follow, then, that no general
pressure should be put upon the Retreatants to make resolutions, unless there is
occasion to suggest some of a very definite
nature relating to actual service that they
may undertake to perform. Resolutions
concerning the interior life should only
be suggested in private interviews to

individuals, to meet some very clear and definite personal need.

Few results of Retreat can be more valuable than the redeeming of the sense and practice of thankfulness from the common neglect into which it has fallen. Thankfulness is the true motive power of Christian service and witness, and not, as seems to be widely assumed, a mere matter of temperament. The question is often asked why the Church of to-day, with all its numbers, wealth, and organization, seems to have so little power of winning souls or of influencing the world of human life ; whereas in the early days it displayed in these respects so mighty a force. History gives us the answer quite plainly. The spirit of thankfulness was the secret. Here was a body of people supposed, in popular repute, to be deluded followers of a senseless and impossible religion. But the world found out one thing about them ; they might be persecuted or tortured, but no oppression could take away from them their happy, thankful confidence as children reconciled with God in the Lord Jesus Christ. So men realized that a new power had come into the world, and sought its source and its significance.

Nowadays worry, rather than thankfulness, is a characteristic of Christian people. As a body we seem to the world to hold a religion mainly of troublous problems; as individuals many of us appear to have enough religion to make ourselves miserable with ; and the world has already sufficient worries and miseries of its own. Quicken thankfulness in Christian souls, and the spirit of service and the power of effective witness will alike revive.

It follows from this that the offering of thanksgivings must not appear in the Retreat as a perfunctory ending to a service of intercession. Intercession is a means of realizing the meaning of the kingdom ; thanksgiving brings home the reality of the Unitive Way. Each exercise must have due prominence in its own appropriate place, and both alike must be saved from formality by the guidance of the Conductor.

CHAPTER IV

RETREATS FOR THE EXPERIENCED

IT has already been made clear that, as the practice of Retreat further extends, Conductors will have to deal more and more with very different sorts of people, in Retreats of varying length.

But, of all the distinctions that can be drawn between Retreatants, none is more practically important than that which exists between those who come into Retreat for the first time, especially if they be young folk, and those who have already become to some extent versed in the practice. Too little attention has, thus far, been given to this point. A certain amount of care is generally bestowed upon grouping Retreatants according to age or sex, education or social rank ; but, from the Conductor's point of view, none of these differences matters so much as that in respect of experience of Retreat, for

the application of the principles sketched
in the preceding chapters must differ
widely in the one case from the other. The
procedure calculated to be most helpful
to beginners, especially the young, in
leading them to a profitable use of Retreat
would certainly be found irksome and dis-
turbing by the more experienced. On the
other hand, if a Retreat be conducted on
the lines most suitable to those to whom
it is habitual, the newcomers could hardly
fail to be left at a loss. Conductors should
therefore think out most thoroughly this
call for variety of method ; and parish
priests should, as far as possible, separate
the two classes when arranging groups for
Parochial Retreats. A good plan to adopt,
when one parish cannot expect to fill more
than one Retreat, is for two parishes to
share two Retreats, sending only experienced people to the first, and reserving the
other for their beginners. But, in any
case, when parish priests find themselves,
as must frequently happen, compelled to
include beginners in a Retreat party con-
sisting mainly of the more experienced,
then at least they should give them as
thorough an instruction as possible in the
object and right use of the time before

they allow them to set out upon the venture.

Generally speaking, though this of course is only roughly true, the better-instructed and more experienced people will be found attending Retreats of not less than three days, commonly called ' mid-week,' while the less experienced, and particularly the younger folk, will be met with at those Retreats which have come, not very happily, to be known as ' week-end.' We will adopt, therefore, this division for the sake of convenience, and first consider the work of the Conductor who is called upon to take a Retreat lasting from a Monday evening to the ensuing Friday morning, or longer as the case may be, in which he has to deal with those who have been into Retreat before, and who may be described, generally, as ' well-instructed ' Church people.

In such a case it is quite likely that the Conductor will be informed that the Retreat has been expressly arranged for members of some one profession, or some particular organization. The Retreatants may thus all be teachers, or members of the Mothers' Union; Church councillors, or members of the Church of England

Men's Society. If this be so the Conductor will do well to lay as little emphasis as possible upon the fact, and to deal with those entrusted to his guidance rather upon the basis of their common humanity.

This is an important point, the ignoring of which often detracts from the real value of a Retreat, and indeed not seldom from other spiritual appeals. The preacher at a military service, for instance, who selects 'Put on the whole armour of God' as his text, and 'Fight the good fight' for the subsequent hymn, is committing a psychological blunder. He should remember that his congregation are men before they are soldiers. But this sort of error is much more serious in the present connection, because it is of the very essence of Retreat that human souls, as such, should be brought to realize the meaning of life and the claims of God.

The fundamental verities are the true subject of Retreat, and there is real danger of irrelevance and waste of opportunity by a misplaced regard for what are merely accidental conditions. It must not be forgotten, in spite of some strange modern gospels, that God's essential claim upon mankind is not for various types of service but consecrated personalities. Religion is meant primarily to make man more truly man, and only secondarily to make him more efficient in whatever may be his profession. And it can be said with confidence that even in Retreats for clergy the appeal, in all the earlier stages at least, should be made to them as men. Towards the end, no doubt, it may be fitting to lay stress upon certain aspects of their relation to God as priests of His Church. But nothing is so little profitable as when the Conductor turns a Retreat for clergy into an occasion for a series of lectures on pastoral methods—the right place for which is in the ' schools ' now provided annually in many of our dioceses.

There is probably no class of Retreatant for whom an introductory address can be safely omitted. In the case we are now considering, namely that of the experienced, there may be no need for much explanation of the simplest elements of Retreat. Yet even habitual Retreatants need help and suggestion at the outset, before the actual course of exercises is begun, in order to gain the right attitude and poise of soul ; for so much of the effect of Retreat depends upon the condition of receptivity ; and this ' waiting upon God ' is an art that is singularly little understood.

In the first place some persons will be found who need to be advised as to the necessity of deliberate mental inhibition at the outset. Earthly worries are fatal to a quiet mind ; and, if the Retreat is to be the eventual solution of any anxiety, this cannot be forced in its first hours. Yet there are some people who come into Retreat, if they only knew it, not so much to find the will of God and true spiritual healing, as to secure for themselves the sort of relief they think they ought to have from their doubts and cares. They start wrong, by worrying rather than waiting. But exterior silence is powerless apart from interior calm ; and the practice of mental inhibition (far too little taught as a condition of spiritual growth) must be impressed upon them as a necessity in order that they may shed mere worries at the threshold of Retreat. A farmer's wife, who knew much responsibility and many sorrows, was once asked to explain her habitually radiant countenance. ' I think,' she replied, ' it is because I learned long ago the secret of never taking my chickens to church.' This is the first secret of a good Retreat, and it will be missed by many if it be not suggested by the Conductor.

Then, again, many devout people seem to be unable to secure this 'waiting upon the Lord,' or to reach a sufficient degree of receptivity, because they imagine that vision comes as the result of much agonizing of soul. They desire a sense of uplift, but by their very earnestness they preclude themselves from gaining it through unconscious counter-suggestion. 'I want illumination ; and I mean to wrestle now in prayer until I get it,' is apt to mean in fact, 'It is difficult to gain, and perhaps hopeless to expect it.' But vision is a privilege granted to patient obedience, rather than the reward of frenzied striving. It is a quiet, receptive frame of mind, in which the emotions come to rest, rather than premature activity, that one should seek to induce at the commencement of Retreat. And the Conductor himself must be careful lest, through a mistaken desire to solemnize the occasion by too much insistence on its critical importance, he brings into the Retreatants' minds a fear of failure, bordering on panic, and remote from the calm of true spiritual attention.

All this has been emphasized at some length because it seems to be so often neglected. Many Conductors are skilled enough in leading the exercises of Retreat, and yet lose heavily in effectiveness through want of care in helping their Retreatants to a right approach.

After the introduction the Conductor's work will be chiefly carried on by way of ' Instructions,' that is to say, the ordering of spiritual truths, and such help and guidance as may be needed for the subsequent meditations of the Retreatants.

It goes without saying that it is by meditation that the fruits of the Retreat will be largely secured ; apart from it the Conductor's instructions will be reduced to the level of emotionally stimulating, or merely interesting, addresses. And the more experienced the Retreatants may be, the more confidently ought the Conductor to be able to rely upon his guidance being thus effectively followed. But alas ! he has only to meet the Retreatants in private interview to find that, quite probably, most of them allege that they do not meditate, cannot meditate, and have given up trying!

H

The truth is that here, again, we labour under the inheritance of a faulty tradition of spiritual training. Much of the teaching of the past, by no means extinct in some popular manuals of devotion, has put into people's minds the idea that nothing is truly meditation unless it takes the form of a sort of advanced spiritual gymnastics, that appears to be quite beyond the reach of ordinary souls. A surprising number of the people we meet in our longer Retreats need almost to be retaught the practice of meditation from the very beginning. They should be shown, therefore, that meditation is not an arbitary and un-natural mental duty required of a Christian, but simply the application to spiritual objects of a natural process, common to all humanity, by which mundane objects, at least, are always attained. We cannot, for instance, make a purchase unless we meditate upon it. We have first to move the mind towards the new coat ; then the desire must come into play—we must wish to obtain the garment. Probably, be it noted, we have already made acts of faith and of repentance ; the tailor is reliable, and we must admit that our failure to make the purchase earlier was the cause of a recent chill. Finally the will comes into action, and we determine upon the acquisition of the garment.

But it should be specially emphasized that in this last process we must will the means as clearly as we will the end, or there can be no actual result. General resolutions would introduce something like lunacy into secular life ; and they are in fact a veritable blight upon spiritual endeavour. We must not only determine to buy the coat ; we must also form, and carry out, the plan of going to the shop and paying the money. Similarly, we must not be content in meditation on spiritual matters with a general resolve to be, let us say, more gentle after the pattern of our Lord ; but must view clearly the next occasion when our self-restraint is likely to be severely tested, and make some practical resolution with that in mind.

People, therefore, should be helped to see that it is simply not true that they cannot meditate. The real truth is that they have, quite probably, not trained themselves with sufficient practical common sense in meditation upon spiritual objects, and are consequently deficient in attainment. It is not the bestowal of a new power that they need, but simply help in the redirection of a faculty which is part of their nature. If a simple form be asked for, as a starting-point, it may be suggested to them that when a truth has been put before them in an address they should ask, and answer, three questions concerning it. ' What does this mean ? ' ' What has it got to do with me ? ' ' Is there anything that I can do about it ? ' This can be made the basis of a meditation that may be real and fruitful, since the questions evoke that movement of the understanding, the desire, and the will which the practice essentially involves. The Conductor, too, should not hesitate, especially in the early stages of the Retreat, to offer some initial guidance in the meditations, putting forward points in short sentences, and suggesting some of the questions, prayers, or acts of faith that they are calculated to evoke. He should then disappear quietly and leave the Retreatants to carry on the exercise in their own way. It is nearly always a mistake to conclude with a hymn, or even with the Grace, since to do so suggests that an end has been reached, when in fact a beginning only has been made.

In Retreats for experienced people the Conductor's advice is often sought in various problems relating to personal life and work. Sometimes the questions raised are by no means easy to answer on the spur of the moment, and the Conductor should not hesitate to ask frankly for time for consideration when it appears to be necessary, and even to be allowed to consult with some one whose judgement or authority are weightier than his own. It can, of course, be easily explained that a case can be stated without the necessity of mentioning names. The need of care and deliberation in dealing with these intimate matters cannot be emphasized too strongly, for much harm has occasionally resulted from the attempt to give a decided but hasty answer in the short space of a single interview.

One of the commonest difficulties, however, in this class of Retreatant arises from the experience of aridity in spiritual things. 'How can I regain joy in my communions and prayers?' is the burden of many forms of question. This spiritual trouble may, of course, arise from various causes, and in any given case the Conductor must be at pains to discover which is involved, or he may commit serious error in his advice. But most frequently the trouble arises from a spiritual form of that ' refusal to grow up ' which the modern psychologists recognize as such a baneful cause of loss in every sphere of life. Souls, having found, in the early stages of spiritual experience, certain modes of satisfaction, desire nothing else but to cling to them. They need to be reminded that the mere desire of ' sensible satisfaction ' belongs to the babyhood of religion, and that a purer way of self-offering is a necessary part of education in sainthood. S. Theresa somewhere speaks of souls complaining in aridity, and supposing that all is lost, when ' the very angels are laughing with joy because God has taken one more soul out of its swaddling-clothes.'

It is the crudest mistake to suppose that no spiritual advance is being made unless there is consciousness of joy. In many lives most happens through times—sometimes long and trying times—of sheer faithful persistence. Joy in the Lord is indeed the reward ; but it is a quieter, deeper, and more effective joy than that which belongs to the early enthusiasms of the newly awakened soul.   And many can testify that, when they were weary to the point of despair, it was a Retreat (and be it said a wise Conductor) that brought them out again into a green pasture.

CHAPTER V

SHORT RETREATS FOR BEGINNERS

THE essential elements of Retreat, as has been shown, are simple and constant, since the fundamental terms of all Retreats are God, stillness, and the human soul. But there is so great a difference between the methods of applying the principles of Retreat to experienced people and that which is required for beginners, especially the young, that these two branches of the Conductor's work may be said almost to constitute two distinct arts. In both cases deeper realization is the object in view. But whereas with more experienced people meditation is the principal, though by no means the only, way of attainment, in the case of the young far more reliance should be placed on what may be called ' expression work.' It is by the actual use of their own spiritual faculties in worship and intercession, in prayer and thanksgiving, and not by over-much explanation concerning the nature of these operations, that children, adolescents, and older people who are, from any cause, newcomers to the way of faith, can best be led to that more vivid ' God-consciousness ' which is so often, as the result of a first Retreat, a turning-point in life.

It is beyond question that many beginners come in this way to a sort of awakening to the fact that spiritual faculties are their own real possession, and that it is a joy to use them. So there is more reality to them thenceforward in the content of religion ; and, specially important in the case of children, enjoyment is associated with the activities of the soul instead of with the various treats or social advantages by which, as they suspect, their pastors and teachers seek to palliate the dreariness of religion itself.

Now this very special character of the art of conducting Retreats for beginners brings with it one distinct advantage. It enables the Church to draw Conductors from a much wider field than would otherwise be the case. Longer Retreats for priests and well-instructed people require for guidance the services of men who have not only a thorough grip of the principles of Retreat, but who are also well versed in such matters as moral theology, and capable of giving sound advice concerning difficult personal problems. But short Retreats for beginners call for a different range of gifts, and indeed of temperaments, in the Conductors. This is true to such a degree that the expert of the long Retreat is often sadly at a loss when confronted with beginners. For what is here required is not so much long training and special knowledge, as a sympathetic understanding of the outlook and difficulties, capacities and limitations, of simple minds, and some measure of readiness and adaptability in the mind of the Conductor himself. Priests who have these sorts of gifts we may thankfully acknowledge that the Church possesses in every town and many a village. We only need to secure among them a wider understanding of the power and possibilities of Retreat, and also of the real joy and refreshment that the hard-worked parish priest can find in conducting them, to secure that the great opportunity will not be lost from want of men ready to seize the occasion.

The Conductor, therefore, of a short Retreat for beginners will have his time-table carefully prepared so as to provide a suitable and duly balanced course of spiritual exercises. He will see to it that, the time being very short, none of it is allowed to be wasted (for even recreation in Retreat is not a waste of time), remembering that his Retreatants need not merely the help of his addresses in chapel, but suggestion and, still more, guidance in the use of the intervals between the services. The time-table itself should provide some definite way of employment for every hour. He will be particularly careful, also, to see that really suitable books are available, for not every Retreat House library can be depended upon to provide them for the young. And he will appoint definite times for the preparation of whatever he desires in the way of intercessions, thanksgivings, or resolutions as to life or service, and not make the mistake of suggesting the performance of these duties at no particular time.

It is very desirable that, in order that this guidance and supervision may be thorough, there should be with the Conductor a specially appointed Helper ; in

Retreats for children, indeed, such assistance is essential. This Helper may be either a man or a woman; many admirably efficient ones of either sex are known to the present writer, who would indeed not dream himself of conducting a Retreat for young people without their co-operation. But, whichever be the sex, this Helper must possess, or be able soon to win, the confidence of the Retreatants, and must have a thorough understanding of the Conductor's aim and methods.

This office, indeed, is rather like that of a Greek Chorus, partly actor and partly audience. For the Helper should be with the Retreatants almost as one of themselves, and sharing their experience ; yet at the same time he must be ready where necessary to interpret the Conductor's directions as to the use of the time in the Common Room or during Recreation. He must be tactful and unobtrusive ; yet able to set the Retreatants at their ease, especially in the early stages of Retreat, in those manifold details out of which diffidence and embarrassment so easily arise, and which are quite outside the Conductor's proper sphere of control. In the case of young people, or those of but little education, the Helper should be ready, whenever it may seem desirable, to read aloud in the Common Room ; for many profit far more by listening than by the attempt to read to themselves. Many a difficulty, too, that might have ended by spoiling the Retreat for more than one, can be solved by the Helper before it has become serious. Many a private interview, looked back upon with thankfulness, may be brought about, because the Helper has been able to dispel the terrors that lurk for the shy Retreatant round the threshold of the Conductor's room.

This office of Helper is by no means easy to fulfil. But it contributes so incalculably to the effectiveness of a short Retreat that not a few of our more adventurous lay people are finding in it nothing short of a new way of spiritual vocation in which they are doing excellent service.

When ample time has been allowed for the settling-in process, and the Retreat actually begins, the Conductor will not fail to give a most thorough explanation of the purpose of Retreat and the conditions necessary to achieve it. The time, no doubt, will come when reliance can be placed upon the parish clergy to have given all this to the people before they come ; at present this cannot normally be expected to have taken place. Most who come into Retreat for the first time require to be told very plainly the sort of things that have been dealt with in the earlier chapters of this book concerning withdrawal, silence, and the example of our Lord.   Anything like abstruse psychological disquisitions must, of course, be avoided ; but there should always be a clear setting forth of the principles chiefly by means of concrete illustrations.   The sort of people usually found in short Retreats come, it must be remembered, from conditions of life in which solitude and silence are regarded as terrors to be shunned, and their minds need a complete redirection towards their sovereign worth.

Again, nearly all English people are inclined to resent a rule that is not understood, so that it is worse than useless, because it provokes antagonism, to give out, as in a notice in church, that silence will be observed. People should be shown, rather, the reasonableness of its necessity in Retreat.   If the value of silence is explained to them, and they are encouraged to face its initial difficulty for the purpose of learning a great secret of life ; if too an appeal is made to be considerate for the sake of others as well as thorough for their own, they will respond readily enough with but few exceptions—and even they can be brought round by special attention from the Helper.

But the effective note for the Conductor to strike is that of encouragement to make a great discovery rather than obedience to a mere rule ; and it is surprising to find how many young people, even of the noisiest ages and types, can be wisely led to the realization of the value of silence, so that they will come back for their second Retreat without the slightest dis-position to talk. If breaks from the silence be allowed, and they may be held to be advisable for many of the very young folk, it should be remembered that the time should be divided into strict silence and reasonable noise. The one thing to avoid at all costs is to have children hang-ing about in ' smudged ' silence and Puritanical gloom. But simple play— with balls, skipping-ropes, etc.—is to be preferred to regularly organized games, since these are apt to loom too large in the memory of Retreat.

Passing now to the actual exercises of the Retreat a word should be said here first upon the paramount importance of worship. Untold harm has been done in the Church's outlook upon evangelization through the widespread disposition to regard worship as the pinnacle of the devout life, rather than the first real step of every soul in its approach to God. And this has gravely affected our idea of Retreats. It is supposed that rapt adoration may be expected of the advanced and experienced, but that younger and simpler folk should be taught a ' practical Christianity,' which is, so strangely, contrasted in many minds with the life of worship.

Now it needs to be realized that godlessness is only very rarely the result of atheism ; generally it proceeds from the extraordinary, yet common, belief in a God Who does not very much matter. This is especially true of the present-day religious outlook in England, and largely determines the atmosphere from which come the sort of Retreatants we are considering now. They are not predisposed to deliberate unbelief, but are rather spiritually unaware of the divine claims upon life, because they have never been

brought to a realization of the Majesty of
God. The one thing that goes to the root
of the whole matter, obviously, is worship
—attributing to God the 'worth' that is
His due. And there is a special character
about the worship of Retreat which in-
creases its value, namely, that it makes a
direct personal demand. In Church services the lukewarm mind of young or old
can, as it were, escape in the crowd.
Services can be habitually attended ; yet
there can be an equally persistent stopping
short of the personal transaction of worship. Children, let it be remarked, are
specially adept at being present with the
body and absent in the mind. Now in
Retreat the priceless element for a personal
decision is introduced. The claim of God
for adoration must be responded to or
deliberately refused ; it can hardly be
simply ignored. This is why so many, in
later years, realize that the act of worship
in their first Retreat was a crisis in their
lives ; and this is the justification held
very strongly by the writer that no Retreat
for beginners is at all likely to be satisfactory that does not provide opportunity
very amply for joining in the Eucharistic
Offering.

I

Mr. J. E. Wareham, in a chapter contributed to *Retreats*, published by the S.P.C.K., has written thus : ' Of the value of a sung Eucharist on the Sunday morning of Retreat, and possibly on some of the other mornings, I am firmly convinced. It can be of a very simple character, and it should be so if the Retreatants are not accustomed to it. Whatever may be the case at other times it is well that in Retreat the whole attention of the Retreatants should be given, at the first service of the day, to the reception of the Holy Sacrament, and that there should be a second service at which their whole attention can be given to worship.'

It is impossible to exaggerate the importance of this advice. The need is far greater than is ordinarily realized of safeguarding souls in the early stages of experience against what are in reality selfish views of the Sacrament of the Altar —the notion, for example, that it was ordained in order that we might receive rather than offer. To exclude the element of worship is to risk perpetuating such errors, and certainly to imperil the effect of the whole Retreat. And, whatever may be the eventual and ideal synthesis, it is a plain fact that common conceptions of worship have sunk so low among us that few of our less instructed folk are capable of realizing deeply both the Gift promised and the adoration that is due at one and the same time.   As we would show a cathedral aspect by aspect, separately, in order that its grandeur as a whole may be revealed to the beholder, so in Retreat we emphasize distinctly the two main aspects of the one great Service of our Lord.

CHAPTER VI

SHORT RETREATS FOR BEGINNERS
(*continued*)

MEDITATION, it has been suggested, should as a formal exercise figure less in a Retreat for young people than in one for their elders. But, reduced to shorter spaces of time, it is by no means unimportant, and presents far less difficulty than might be supposed. This is no doubt because for the young it remains a natural function, and has not yet been confused by past failures or obscured by technicalities derived from books of devotion. Beginners will be found, as a rule, not only to apprehend easily the points presented to them in an instruction, but also to follow simple guidance in subsequent devotion with real profit, and it is far better to teach them to meditate by helping them to do it than by much explanation of the practice.

In the mode of this guidance much depends on the Conductor's personal temperament and gifts, for here, if anywhere, he must be a personal leader and not merely a technical teacher. But, generally, a good plan is to rely chiefly on the repetition of short key-phrases, with devotional and suggestive comments, and short spaces of silence. Thus ' I come from God ' is repeated after the Conductor ; then follows a moment of silence ; a quiet comment is made by the Conductor; then, after another few seconds of silence, the phrase is repeated again. This may be done two or three times, and then other phrases such as ' I belong to God,' ' I go to God,' can be dealt with in the same sort of way.

Young Retreatants should not be left to kneel for indefinite periods. The Helper, after a reasonable interval following the Conductor's departure, should himself rise and leave the chapel, explaining at some suitable time that Retreatants may follow or not as they wish.

As regards the instructions to be given, it has to be remembered, once more, that these are not in themselves the main object but a means towards it. Consequently the Conductor's methods must be adaptable to the actual circumstances, and not determined by the supposed necessities of a rigid scheme. It is often advisable, when young people are obviously getting on well in their own devotions, not to give an address that has been contemplated ; it happens, hardly less often, that one becomes necessary at an unexpected point to help them to regain spiritual attention. Numerous short addresses, especially of an explanatory sort, are more likely to be effective than a few longer ones, which is certainly not the case in Retreats for really experienced people, provided of course that due limits are observed.

It must be remembered, too, that only the trained mind (and even that by no means always) works by strictly rational processes ; consequently progressive ideas should be set before beginners as much as possible by way of striking associations rather than by much logical argument. The biologist, for example, may lecture on ' The salmon ; its structure ; its habitat.' But children, and we ourselves when we are not on our guard, are much more apt to be thinking ' salmon ; fish-monger's shop ; the cat there has kittens ;

I want the black one.' The wise teacher will not simply deplore this tendency and neglect it in his methods, but will make no small use of it for instruction. It must be remembered that a parable is, after all, the imparting of spiritual truth not by rational argument but by vivid association with a familiar fact.

A large element in this art consists in the skilful use of illustrations ; only these must really illustrate, and must not be themselves the sole focus-point of attention and memory.

Before we dismiss the subject of instruction let this be emphasized very strongly—it is necessary to be simple ; *but simplicity is not triviality*. This is where not only some Conductors, but many preachers, meet with disaster ; in their efforts to speak within the terms of limited minds they discourse upon subjects that are of no very great importance to anybody. Children, and almost illiterate elders, are remarkably quick to realize when they are thus ' being talked down to.' Inwardly they resent it, and the sympathy between preacher and people is immediately lost. In a Beginners' Retreat there is certainly more necessity than elsewhere for explanations of details ; but, apart from that, the subjects dealt with in the instructions should be as fundamental as though all the Retreatants were university professors.

But a Conductor may be a past-master of simple instruction and will even then fail with beginners unless he realizes the immense power of suggestion, and is quick to seize opportunities for its effect. It has been pithily remarked that ' the devil is an expert psychologist.' Temptations rarely take the form of abstract explanations of the delights of sinfulness ; souls are generally lured to their ruin by the suggestions that emanate from black bottles, cards, gold, evil pictures, or bad company. On the other side, the coming of the kingdom of God is sadly hindered by the sheer secularity of our modern life ; the importance of suggestion has been so little taken into account that it is fatally easy nowadays, as distinct from former ages, for men to grow from infancy to maturity in homes, schools, and factories —or, no less, palaces—in which there are almost no suggestions at all of the spiritual and the holy. The surface of their minds may, with luck, be now and then subject

to the impression of some religious appeal;
but the background of their minds, which
is all important, is rarely subject to any
quiet force of influence from sight or
sound of the things that belong unto their
souls' peace.   So a Retreat, especially for
the young, is bound to fail if admirable
instructions are given upon a background
of negative, or contrary, suggestion. Here
is the need for brightness instead of drab-
ness, vivacity in place of repression, in the
arrangements of the House ; for reverent
beauty in the chapel, and especially in the
ceremonial of the Eucharist.   But there
are many other ways in which this power
of suggestion can be employed, and the
wise Conductor will be always on the look-
out in order to learn them.   They are too
numerous to be dealt with now, but one
in particular may be selected as an important example, and that is the ' Procession
to Calvary.'

In that part of a short Retreat which
deals with the Cross and Passion, time
and the Retreatants' own limited powers
forbid a long and detailed exposition of
the doctrine of the Atonement.   But a
procession can be made, while a hymn or
litany is sung, to a Calvary (or a sacred

picture hung for the purpose upon a tree) in the garden. Short devotions are there conducted before the Cross, ending, perhaps, with another hymn, and certainly with a few moments of silence. It will be found that no better introduction could be desired for the ensuing instruction and meditation upon the penitential life, for the force of suggestion will most powerfully have worked in the minds of not a few.

Lastly, attention is directed to the ' Conference on ways of serving God,' suggested in the appended time-table. This needs a word of explanation. Conferences in Retreat are rightly depreciated by most Conductors. They break into the devotional course, even when they are supposed to deal with devotional matters; furthermore, those Retreatants least capable of helping the others are apt to become the most prominent, with the result of unprofitable irrelevance. But, in the writer's opinion, when young people all come from the same parish it is sometimes advisable to have a very short conference, which can be directed by the Helper though started by the Conductor, which must be strictly confined to the subject

' What can we do when we get back ? '
Young people so often are willing to serve,
but, since they cannot be Sunday school
teachers or district visitors, they do not
know what to do, and their desire never
reaches fruition. A conference of a few
minutes, especially if the Helper knows
his business, may easily lead to pledges of
service for a definite object, which, if
desired, can be offered upon the altar at
the final service of the Retreat. Detailed
discussion can be left for a subsequent
meeting in the parish, and only the main
intention decided in the Retreat.

This conference should not be regarded
as a rule ; it is often inadvisable or unnecessary to hold it. On the other hand,
it has not infrequently led quite directly
to some of the most marked and astonishing of the results that parishes have
derived from the venture of a Retreat for
beginners.

CHAPTER VII

SOME FINAL SUGGESTIONS

IN every walk of life, as is well known, the expert appears to have all the luck; the bungler to be the unfortunate victim of circumstances beyond his control. The complete angler, for example, comes home with a full basket and a cheerful countenance ; the beginner returns from the same river unladen and yet weary. Question the latter and you will hear a gloomy tale of weather conditions that no human skill could circumvent ; of fish that knew no hunger ; of the unexpected call for some special tackle that none could have foreseen.

In reality sheer luck has very little to do with the matter. The good fortune of the experienced fisherman has been derived from the fact that he understood the weather conditions, appreciated their probable influence on the feeding habits of the fish, and decided rightly what size of fly, length of cast, balance of rod, and weight of line were appropriate for the day.

Now it is very noteworthy that, in Retreat, smoothness of running is one of the surest signs of the master-hand at work. The expert Conductor seems to be largely immune from misfortune, while the less skilful meet with hitch after hitch to their own heavy discouragement. But once more luck has but little part in causing the difference. The truth is that the expert Conductor knows that a Retreat is peculiarly sensitive to certain conditions, and that such as are adverse may seriously impair its success. But he knows, too, that he has one great advantage over the invited speaker at a conference, or preacher in a strange church, in that to no small extent he can modify the conditions, or at least make special arrangements to meet such as are difficult.

Exactly, therefore, as the skill of the angler is at work not only while he fishes but before he comes to the brink of the stream, so the art of the Conductor must be not only sustained during the Retreat but operative long before its commencement. It cannot be urged too insistently that timely and sustained attention to minute detail is of an importance that can hardly be exaggerated.

The Conductor must, to begin with, get into close touch with the person who is organizing the Retreat. He should require reasonably full information as to the persons who are coming, and secure (instead of merely taking for granted) that they are not utterly incongruous as to age and mental level. Still more urgently should he insist that they shall have been prepared for the Retreat, at least in so far as to have been told that it is definitely a serious occasion, and not a pleasant week-end of liberty and repose. Through neglect of this precaution more than one Conductor has landed himself in an almost impossible situation, which has brought discredit upon the Retreat as a method and serious loss of confidence in himself.

Then, too, he should be careful to arrive at the House not after, but well before the Retreatants. The sight of a bag-laden priest plunging in just as the bell goes for the first service powerfully suggests the very notion that should chiefly be avoided, namely, that all he is concerned with is to give the addresses. Furthermore, if he arrives late he cannot, as he certainly ought, visit the Chapel and the Common Rooms and see that the provision of books and other arrangements are in accordance with his wishes, nor find out in good time what special adaptation of his plan may be necessary for the convenience of the staff. Last, but not least, unless he arrives early he cannot establish a sense of friendly and confident co-operation, at least with the leaders of the staff, before they are involved in the strain of their absorbing duties.

Then it should be remembered that these same members of the staff are not only anxious, for the credit of their House, to secure the comfort of the Retreatants, but are further quite ready to receive from the Conductor directions, even as to household matters, that are tactfully given. When mistakes occur it is generally because some one has been left in ignorance until too late to provide a remedy. If a Common Room, for instance, has become too cold—or even more disastrously the Chapel—it is probably not due to a mistaken desire to save fuel, but to the fact that the staff has been busy elsewhere, and the Retreatants too shy to suggest improvement.

It may be impossible, for more than one reason, to choose hymns beforehand, and there are indeed types of Retreats in which hymns are altogether out of place. But for most Retreats hymns can be used with advantage, if they strike an objective note and are not sentimental and unduly introspective. But, even if they are selected after arrival, they must not be hastily chosen, for it is better to have no hymns at all than unsuitable ones. In the case of young people especially a preliminary choir practice is particularly desirable, since it affords both a gradual approach to the actual Retreat, and an opportunity for many notices and explanations that, at a later stage, might seriously break into the atmosphere of devotion.

A large measure of liturgical freedom should be claimed by the Conductor, and will not be refused, except of course in the case of those Community Houses in which the regular offices form a part of the Retreat. Psalms and lessons, however, in other cases should be expressly and carefully chosen to fit in with the spiritual exercise in hand and the tenour of the address. To reduce the services to the level of irrelevant preliminaries is an error which may easily result from a precise following of the order for the day in the Prayer Book.

Sometimes a Conductor is tempted to seek a point of contact with the Retreatants by consulting them as to arrangements. This practice is nearly always a mistake, since it results most probably in instilling a loss of confidence as to his own power of guidance.

Punctuality on the part of the Conductor is of the utmost importance. He should never commence a service before the stated time ; still less, after the bell has rung, should he keep the Retreatants waiting. On no account should he lose touch with the clock during an address, which should never exceed forty minutes ; nor should he carry on services late at night, a remark which applies with greater force to the matter of interviews.

In the intervals the Conductor should not be satisfied with having told the Retreatants what to do, but assure himself that they know how to carry out his suggestions, and also have the necessary means—in the shape of books, or pencils and paper, as the case may be. For instance, a bare injunction to young

K

people to prepare their intercessions will lead only to blankness of mind, whereas the provision of papers marked with appropriate headings, such as ' My home and friends,' ' My parish,' ' Our country,' ' The world,' will not seldom let loose a stream of interesting and intelligent requests.

Finally, the advice that the young Conductor stands as a rule most in need of, especially in dealing with beginners, is to trust boldly and effectually to the Holy Spirit working upon souls in the great main conditions of Retreat. Some often fail because the difficulties of shyness, unfamiliarity, and so on, that are apt to be felt in the very early stages, cause them a certain loss of nerve. They fear too much that the Retreatants will not find calmness and joy but will become restless and bored. So they themselves begin to look anxious and distressed, and may be tempted from the true aim of letting the power of seclusion and silence find its way through the troubled surface, and try instead to save disaster by means of interesting addresses, relaxation of rules, or— worst of all—services of a ' bright and hearty ' description.

They need to remind themselves again and again of the foundation truth that man is by nature a spiritual being ; that all souls, even drawn from the most unlikely circumstances, have faculties for apprehending the spiritual and laying hold upon God ; and that all through the ages of religious history it has been shown that silence and seclusion are great natural conditions in which most surely these faculties wake into life.

Many a Retreat that has begun in uncertainty and trepidation has ended as a thing of power and joy, simply because the Conductor has known how to be faithful to true ideals and to the principles of his most honourable art and service.

APPENDICES

I (*A*). Time-table for a Three-Day Retreat for experienced people.

  (*B*). Time-table for a Week-end Retreat for beginners.

II. Headings for addresses following the main lines of the *Spiritual Exercises* of S. Ignatius.

APPENDIX I (*A*)

*A suggested Time-Table for a Three-Day Retreat
for Experienced People.*

FIRST DAY.
- 7.30. Supper.
- 9. 0. Compline.   Introductory Address.

SECOND, THIRD, AND FOURTH DAY.
- 8. 0. Holy Communion.
- 8.45. Breakfast.
- 10.15. Instruction and Meditation.
- 12.15. Sext.   Intercessions.
- 1. 0. Dinner.

RECREATION

- 4. 0. Tea.
- 4.30. Instruction and Meditation.
- 6.45. Evensong.   Thanksgivings.
- 7.30. Supper.
- 9. 0 Compline.   Summing up of points ;
  short guided Devotions ; Meditation.

FIFTH DAY.
- Holy Communion.
- Breakfast.

NOTE.—It will be seen from the above time-table that (*a*) two full and careful instructions are regarded as sufficient for each day ; (*b*) ample time is left for private meditation ; and (*c*) opportunity is provided for an interview with each Retreatant to be fitted in.

APPENDIX I (B)

A suggested Time-Table for a Week-end Retreat for Beginners.

SATURDAY.

4.15. Choir Practice.

5. 0. Tea.

6.15. Evensong. Introductory Address. Silence begins.

7.30. Supper.

8.15. Preparation of Intercessions.

9. 0. Compline. Short Instruction and Meditation. } The Foundation.

SUNDAY.

8. 0. Holy Communion.

8.45. Breakfast.

9.45. Devotional Reading in Common [Room.

10.15. Choral Eucharist. Short Address. } The Kingdom.

12.15. Short Address. Intercessions.

1. 0. Dinner.

RECREATION.

3.45. Procession to Calvary. } The Passion.

4. 0. Instruction and Meditation.

5. 0. Tea.

5.30. Preparation of Thanksgivings.

6.15. Evensong. Instruction and Medi-[tation.

7.30. Supper.

8. 0. Conference on ways of serving God. } The Life of Grace.

8.45. Offering of Resolutions. Compline. Thanksgivings.

MONDAY.

Holy Communion.

Breakfast.

Silence will be observed in the House and Grounds from the first Evensong till the last Holy Communion.

NOTES ON THE FOREGOING TIME-TABLE

The headings in the last column indicate the main stages of the Ignatian sequence of ideas.

The Choir Practice is useful, not only for the preparation of music, but also for a gradual entry into the experience of Retreat ; for giving out necessary notices ; and, not least, for a word on the necessity of worship (cf. page 112).

The address at Evensong should be an explanation of the purpose of Retreat (cf. page 12).

For the preparation of Intercessions see page 85.

The instruction after Compline should be on some fundamental point, e.g. the purpose and destiny of life.

The devotional reading on the Sunday morning may be conducted by the Helper.

Before the Eucharist the Conductor, or an assistant priest, may lead the preparation, and afterwards the thanksgivings.

The address may be upon worship ; the Eucharistic Sacrifice ; the glory and call of the kingdom (cf. page 73).

A short address may fitly be given before the Intercessions concerning the life of prayer.

The object of the procession to Calvary (which may be represented by a picture or crucifix hung upon a tree if no Calvary be in the grounds) is to make a vivid presentation to the mind of the fact of our Lord's Passion. Hymns or a Litany should be sung in a procession starting from the

Chapel, and short devotions conducted before the Calvary. The subsequent Instruction and Meditation in the Chapel should be on some aspect of the penitential life.

For preparation of Thanksgivings see page 88.

The Instruction and Meditation after Evensong should be on the doctrine of the Holy Spirit, the Sacraments, rules of life, or some other aspect of the Life of Grace.

For Conference and Resolutions see pages 122 and 87.

APPENDIX II

HEADINGS FOR ADDRESSES

*Following the main lines of the ' Spiritual
Exercises ' of S. Ignatius*

THE following are suggested lines of thought which, in varying modes of expression, may be found useful in conducting Retreats for any class of people.

INTRODUCTORY ADDRESS

Knowing a friend.   The necessity of visits to (*a*) talk, and (*b*) listen, about mutual interests.   *If* friendship be thus maintained short meetings, letters, etc., are kept full of meaning ; otherwise ' casual acquaintance ' supplants friendship.   So with the Divine Friendship ; without Retreat danger of ' conventional religion ' ; with Retreat ordinary devotions retain their meaning.   In the Bible the work of God's kingdom is done not merely by organized religious people but by the friends of God, who were prepared by Retreat.

The conditions of this visit to God are seclusion, for the time must be *devoted* to God ; and silence, for it is hardly ever except in silence that ideas of God and His purpose grow strong enough in the mind to be a motive force.

The object of Retreat should be (*a*) rest and refreshment of body, mind, and spirit ; (*b*) renewed devotion ; and (*c*) a reordering of life. Retreat is the quiet bay where the ship is 'careened' for clearing from weeds and overhauling. Retreat is the mount where we meet our Lord, and also can look down upon the plain and see more clearly just where we have been missing the Way of Life.

> Lord, help us to be still that we may know that Thou art God.
> Lord, help us to serve Thee with all our mind.
> Lord, teach us to pray.

The Foundation

All sensible actions are for an object ; processes without purpose are evidence of insanity. Is life sane or senseless ? What is its object ? Only God. Riches can never buy the things that really matter, and shrouds have no pockets ; pleasures cease to please. Man is a spiritual, eternal being ; only God can satisfy his soul.

This satisfaction must be found now. Here is the call and promise of Jesus Christ—the way of the Cross to find more abundant life. This means that the condition of finding is *detachment*, i.e. not aloofness or remoteness from the world's affairs, but not valuing any earthly thing for its own sake and apart from its eternal values. Men take stones from the same quarry ; some make a road, others a prison-house. So do they with the

' creatures,' i.e. the powers and opportunities of life.

Only as we hear the call and become 'detached' do we see life as it is, cf. a limpet close fixed in a thick shell, lives in illusion, thinking that the ocean is a narrow green stream filled with food ; knowing nothing of its limitless grandeur. So men look on the world as a (rather badly) finished place for them to enjoy, instead of the glorious kingdom in the making. In Retreat we escape from illusion, and recover the eternal values of life. There is no *real* meaning in life apart from God and His kingdom. Life is meant to be a finding of God—but can be made a losing of Him, than which nothing can be more awful to contemplate.

> We come from God.
> We belong to God.
> We go to God.

The Kingdom

(a) The Being and Nature of God.

The soul, finding in Christ the meaning of life, is not called to self-satisfaction, but to the service of the kingdom. To understand the kingdom we must know the King ; for the kingdom is the extension of God's purpose throughout the world ; the impress of the divine character on every sphere of human life. Godlessness comes less often through atheism than through

unworthy ideas of God causing ignorance of, and
indifference to, His kingdom.

Therefore God revealed in Christ is the
starting-point of the kingdom ; and worship,
loving reverence for His holy Name, the first
necessary step in man's acceptance of His reign.
Worship is not, merely, a pinnacle of specially
devout life ; it is the foundation of every simple
and effective Christian life.

In Retreat God must be seen ' high and lifted
up.' We worship before : (1) The Mystery of
God's Being ; (2) His several attributes, e.g.
holiness (purity, perfection), righteousness, justice,
mercy, truth, and above all love (i.e. not a sentimental regard for our present happiness and
comfort, but an eternal will for our real good).
God's only aim for humanity, and each one of us,
is our perfection in His likeness. We are to be
as ' perfect ' in our nature and capacities as God
is in His.[1] But if worship is not the mainstay
of our life we do not advance in knowledge,
offering, service of God.

> Holy, holy, holy, Lord God of Hosts.
> Heaven and earth are full of Thy glory.
> Glory be to Thee, O Lord most High.

(b) The Atoning Sacrifice.

We could have no part or lot in the kingdom
but for our Lord's redeeming Sacrifice. 'Sacrifice'
is a word much misused in common speech ; it

[1] S. Matt. v. 48.

does not mean loss, but consecration. So all our Lord's work, in time and eternity, for our sakes, is ' sacrifice.' The Cross represents it because it signifies the occasion of the full giving of His life.

Sacrifice is not solely a Jewish invention, but the age-long core of religion. When man draws near to God it is right that he should bring a gift. But this is not to ' buy off ' God's anger. That is the distortion, not the primary root of the idea of sacrifice ; which is rather : man is alienated from God by his transgression ; in that which is offered God and man share, and so Atonement is found. Thus in the main stream of the idea of sacrifice we see ' offering ' and ' communion ' as two essential aspects of the same transaction.

Spiritual selfishness is a danger in the life of the communicant, e.g. seeking *only* grace for *our* needs. We must remember the memorial of Calvary, and the offering of the eternal Sacrifice by our great High Priest. In union with Him we offer ourselves, our souls and bodies.

> O saving Victim, opening wide,
>   The gate of heaven to man below ;
> Our foes press hard on every side,
>   Thine aid supply, Thy strength bestow.

(c) Intercession.

It is easy in the life of prayer to slip into the way of regarding ' our prayers ' as if they were only the ' duty ' of expressing religious sentiments.

So people ask us : ' How can what *you say* interfere with the laws of nature, or bring anything to pass that would not otherwise happen ? '

But we live by using powers entrusted to us to affect the course of events, e.g. walking, holding a book that by ' the laws of nature ' ought to fall, etc. Prayer is the greatest power we possess. It is the power by which we (*a*) bring our wills into harmony with the divine will, and (*b*) keep human life open for the power of God to work in it.

The story of the Bible is of God's power waiting on God's people for them to claim and use. When they are faithful and claim the power in prayer, the works of the kingdom are carried out. When they are faithless and do not pray, life is shut up against the power of God—cf. the Acts of the Apostles, that might almost be called the Acts of the Holy Ghost, because of faithful prayer. So, in Retreat, by interceding with our great High Priest, we can realize the kingdom more deeply than by hearing it explained.

Thy kingdom come. Thy will be done, in earth as it is in heaven.

Thou, O Lord, art in the midst of us, and we are called by Thy Name. Leave us not, O Lord, our God.

The Passion

(*a*) *The Cross.*

It is only when we have worshipped the King that we can realize the Passion. The Cross signifies not, as the world so often supposes, the cruel death of a beautiful Teacher, but the full and willing giving of His life by the Incarnate Son of God. No less than He, the King of Glory, gave Himself on the Cross for us.

The meaning of the Cross cannot be fully explained. The fact of the Cross must make its own deep, silent appeal to each soul. But we can understand that (*a*) saving love must suffer, (*b*) that Jesus Christ's all-holy life could not have been *wholly* offered for us but through death, (*c*) that without the Cross we could not know Him as Saviour, nor (*d*) understand the meaning of the Way of the Cross in human life, nor (*e*) realize fully the meaning of the love of God.

Many go to Bethlehem, but few go on to Calvary. There is some readiness nowadays in the world to admit the need of religion in life, and to want to know about our Lord's teaching. But there is as much blindness as ever to the need of redemption. Men want a Christianity to stimulate ideals ; a religion to make imperfect man a little better. But man needs saving, not only improving. Only the religion of the Cross can meet our real need ; nothing short of acknowledgement of Jesus Christ *as Saviour* can bring to us the enthusiasm of thankfulness which is the only sufficient motive for the service of God. We cannot understand God, or deeply love Him, till we have taken into our hearts the message of the Cross

L

Saviour of the world, Who by Thy Cross and
precious Blood hast redeemed us,
Save us and help us, we humbly beseech Thee, O
Lord.

(b) *The Penitential Life.*

Before the Cross we need to think of sinfulness
rather than only of sins. The Church's faith
concerning sin is not that there is a black list of
things we may not do, but that there is in human
nature a *corruption of motive* which can impress a
mark of sinfulness on any sort of action—cf. our
Lord's teaching in S. Matthew.

Sin is essentially the rebellion of the will against
God. It leads to separation from God, not
because if we do many wrong things God will be
angry, but because *by its own action* it destroys
in us our nature of childhood so that we cannot
dwell with God ; as strong acid destroys a garment, or dry-rot woodwork. Sin seems to offer
freedom ; but it results in exchanging the loving
service of the Father, which is the only true
freedom, for the pitiless tyranny of the lord of
the far country. Sin is always waste ; *not* the
contracting of evil faculties in place of good ones,
but the *misuse* of the powers of our nature which
in themselves are good.

True penitence does not only look back with
sorrow, but forward with resolve. Penitence is
coming back to God by the way of the Cross ;
and confession is not telling God our sins (He

knows them already), but owning them before the Cross in order to disown our allegiance to them. Not the emotion of sorrow, but the persistence of the will in the ' return journey,' is the measure of our penitence. For sin we need two things : (*a*) forgiveness by which we are assured of God's full acceptance of us for a fresh beginning ; (*b*) power to overcome. In Christ, and because of His Cross, both are pledged to the repentant soul. Thus penitence is the only condition of joy and of victory.

NOTE.—An instruction on these lines may be given by means of a simple Bible-reading on the Parable of the Prodigal Son, drawing attention to such points as the following : ' Give me '—the root of selfishness ; ' goods '—the evil was not in them, but in their misuse ; ' took his journey ' —the rebellion necessitated separation ; ' wasted his goods '—see above ; ' began to be in want '— the satisfaction of sin is always a passing illusion ; ' went and hired himself '—he did not find freedom, but slavery ; ' came to himself '—the opposite of ' ecstasy,' showing not emotional excitement, but the sane action of the will ; ' arise and go '—the persistent effort to make the journey, so much more difficult in the return than in going down to the far country. The hardship and humiliation of walking it step by step, ragged and famished. ' Kissed him '—restoration to his sonship, not because the father had been angry and was then pacified, but because forgiveness had been made possible by the son's return.

The Cross is God's witness against sin.
The Cross is God's remedy for sin.

The Unitive Way

(a) *The Doctrine of the Holy Ghost.*

The danger of 'dualism'; so often people think and speak as if the 'spiritual,' 'the heavenly,' 'the eternal,' signified a sphere different from, and even opposed to, the 'material,' 'the earthly,' 'the temporal.' But the world was made to be the habitation and expression of the spiritual; human life, here and now, is meant to be not only God-created, but God-inspired and God-possessed.

The confusion and disorder of sin. The world made unfit to be the dwelling-place of the Holy Spirit. The work of re-creation in the Incarnation. The perfect Manhood of our Lord was consummated by the Ascension, then (but not till then) could the Holy Ghost, Who fulfils in us His presence, indwell in the Body of Christ. Thus the Church is not a society of people hedged in for their own salvation, but the focus-point of God's redeeming power; the instrument of the kingdom. Hence the seriousness of post-baptismal sin hindering the purpose of God.

The Spirit-bearing Body. Its privileges; its claim for the loyalty and enthusiasm of its members; its responsibilities. The events of the time are proving the fact of the interdependence of mankind. The Church is called to show to the world the real meaning of brotherhood in service. Its need of enlightenment, power, love.

> Source of life, Who fillest all the world,
>   We worship and adore Thee.
> Spirit of light, Who teachest all the truth,
>   We worship and adore Thee.
> Source of all gifts of nature and of grace,
>   Lord and Life-giver,
>   We worship and adore Thee.

(b) Sacramental Life.

The Sacraments, like the Incarnation, come of God's condescension to our real human need. True Fatherhood does not only put before children beautiful ideas, but condescends to the actual needs of the children, e.g. a father does not describe the glories of Canadian cornfields to hungry children, but cuts them slices of bread.

The present danger of ' broad-minded,' i.e. vague religion. The man who seeks God *only* everywhere will end by finding Him really nowhere. By finding God *really* somewhere, i.e. in the appointed sacramental way, we are enabled to find Him everywhere.

The simplicity of the Sacrament of the Altar, which any child can grasp, is as wonderful as its mystery. ' Communion '— we often lose the sense of God's closeness in the coldness and distraction of the world, and regain that sense in a devout communion. ' Bread and wine '— food and refreshment ; renewal of strength. Christian life is a thing of conflict and effort in which we grow weary. In our communions we are strengthened again by the imparting of the power of our Lord's all-holy life. It is not the duty of making regular communions that should be the centre of our thought, but the privilege of this inestimable means, so completely within our reach, of maintaining the life of communion with God and with each other in Christ.

> Bread of heaven, on Thee we feed,
> For Thy Flesh is meat indeed.
> Vine of heaven, Thy Blood supplies
> This blest cup of sacrifice.
> Thou our life, O may we be
> Rooted, grafted, built on Thee.

Printed by A. R. Mowbray & Co. Ltd., London and Oxford